Thought
this 7
been.
we.
inten... ✓

Best Sue.

ONE LUCKY DEVIL

THE FIRST WORLD WAR MEMOIRS OF
SAMPSON J. GOODFELLOW

SAMPSON J. GOODFELLOW

Edited by
EDWARD WILLETT

SHADOWPAW
PRESS

ONE LUCKY DEVIL:
The First World War Memoirs
of Sampson J. Goodfellow

Text copyright 2018
Estate of Sampson J. Goodfellow
All rights reserved

All images believed to be in public domain.

Cover design by Edward Willett

ISBN 978-1-9993827-6-6
Kindle ISBN 978-1-9993827-7-3
Epub ISBN 978-1-9993827-8-0

Order from:
SHADOWPAW PRESS
303 - 2333 Scarth Street
Regina, Saskatchewan
Canada S4P 2J8

orders@shadowpawpress.com
www.shadowpawpress.com

CONTENTS

FOREWORD

I NEVER MET SAM GOODFELLOW. He died in 1979, when I was at university in Arkansas. After graduation I returned to my home town of Weyburn to work at the *Weyburn Review*, and almost ten years passed before I moved to Regina. But nine years after I arrived in the city, I married Margaret Anne Hodges, P.Eng., Sam's granddaughter, and acquired a wonderful mother-in-law, Dr. Alice Goodfellow —Sam's daughter.

Dr. Goodfellow, who passed away in 2013, lived in the house that Sam and Nancy bought in 1939. Now *I* live in that house, with Margaret Anne and our daughter, also named Alice. A lot of our furniture once belonged to Sam and Nancy, including a wonderful grand piano, and there are knick-knacks and oddments and keepsakes galore that date to their married life, and even before—for example, opera scores that Nancy brought from England. (Some of these formed the basis for a series of spots I did on CBC Saskatchewan's *Afternoon Edition* radio program when Colin Grewar hosted it, called, "Things I Found in My Mother-in-Law's House.")

As a result, I rather felt I *did* know Sam, even before I discovered the memoirs he had written late in life, sometime in the 1970s. Typed up and bound in loose-leaf notebooks, they fascinated me from the beginning with their account of his childhood in Scotland, his early years in Toronto and Regina, and, especially, his service in the Great War.

Ten years ago, I posted these memoirs (at the time, largely unedited) online, on my website, www.edwardwillett.com. But with the arrival of 2018, and with it the centennial of the Armistice that ended the First World War, I decided it was time to act on an idea I'd had from the beginning: to properly edit and release in print form Sam's personal account of his early life and experiences during the war.

Earlier this year I started my own publishing house, Shadowpaw Press, with the thought that this would be one of its earliest releases. And so, here it is: one man's sharply observed account of his service in the war that ended one hundred years ago this November.

I have edited with a light hand, correcting grammar and spelling here and there and making an effort to ensure that place names and other proper nouns are correct (where there's significant uncertainty, I've inserted an editor's note).

But by and large, these are Sam's words, just as these are Sam's experiences.

I hope you find them as fascinating and enlightening as I did, and that you will feel, as do I, that you've met someone you'll remember all your life.

Edward Willett
Regina, Saskatchewan
October 2018

A SCOTTISH CHILDHOOD

One day when I was twelve years old, I said to my mother, "What happened when I was around three or four years old?"

Mother looked at me. "What do you mean? What do you remember?"

"I really don't know," I said, "but something has bothered me for a long time. There seems to have been a great disturbance, a quarrel, a fight, or some misunderstanding. Please tell me what it was."

After a moment, Mother said, "Very well, I'll tell you. It's only right that you should know. The incident you refer to was when your father wanted to go to the United States of America to start a new life. He felt that on account of conditions in Scotland, and with so many others emigrating to America, that it would be the best for you and your brother, and also me. The Americans were opening up their country —they were wanting people for agriculture and manufacturing and more. It was a new country, with greater opportunities for workers, and no class distinction. They wanted pioneers."

But, Mother told me, she had a premonition that if my father went, she would never see him again, that he would either desert her or be killed—and she was correct: she was later informed he had been killed in a rail accident before he could save enough money to send for us. He had been buried in Philadelphia.

Mother said she was surprised I could remember the incident. "It must have made a great impression!"

Mother always seemed to be able to glimpse into the future. Perception or intuition, call it what you will, she always knew what was happening to any of her relatives, and was always correct. At my young age, it seemed very frightening.

Sometimes friends would come to our house to have their fortunes told with playing cards or have their tea leaves or palms read (a common practice at the time when people visited each other's homes). It was lots of fun because I made jokes about it, but when the reading came true, I shivered.

M y father had been the youngest boy of his family and was well and truly spoiled. He could not stand discipline or chastisement, and so he left his home town of Hanley, Staffordshire, and went to Edinburgh, Scotland, where a brother, Fred, was living. That didn't suit him either, so he wandered all over Scotland for a while, before finally returning to Edinburgh.

By all accounts he was a handsome daredevil, always up to some prank with his chums. When his friends—ex-soldiers, sailors, and others—decided they were going to America, of course he wanted to go along—which he did.

As a result, Mother was left with two children, me and my little brother, Fred, two years my junior, to rear and educate. We lived in many different homes under poor conditions, and our health started to fail.

I remember falling sick and being rushed to the hospital with a childhood disease. I remember it not so much because I was sick (it wasn't long before I was out), but because one day Mother brought me a banana. It was the first I had seen, and it tasted wonderful.

Another incident while living in Edinburgh that I remember well was the day we were taken to the sea-side resort of Portobello (remember the school-girl rhyme in *The Pride of Miss Jean Brodie*, "Edinburgh, Leith, Portobello, Musselburgh, and Dalkeith?"). Whoever took us did not know that children left alone have the habit of wandering, which Fred and I did.

Our wandering ended when we were picked up by the local policemen and taken to the police station. The police at the station had lots of fun with us. I can remember (as if it were yesterday) them buying us ice cream—or it may have been hokey pokey (penny a lump!). When Mother got in touch with the police, they hated to see us go because they were having so much fun amusing us.

Portobello Beach, ca. 1900 (City of Edinburgh Council).

I can also remember going to Holyrood Palace, which at that time was a soldiers' barracks. The soldiers, too, would have lots of fun with us, and give us a penny.

Finally, Mother decided we had to leave Edinburgh. After she saw an advertisement in *The Scotsman* newspaper, we were taken to Langside Cottage, in the country outside of Dalkeith.

Langside Farm Cottage near Dalkeith (seen here in Google Street View). This may be the same cottage, or at least in the same location.

It was a lovely place. You came up a grade from Dalkeith, with a forest on the righthand side and farmers' fields on the left. At the corner was a rise of ground where I used to lie, dreaming about what I would do when I grew up, my imagination running wild (although I never thought I would go to Canada, since I didn't know there was such a place!).

On Saturday and Sunday, the poachers would come out with their hounds to chase the rabbits—provided the gamekeeper was not around. If the gamekeeper appeared, they would chain up their dogs, leaving the gamekeeper with no proof they were poaching—they just said they were exercising their dogs.

The land belonged to the Duke of Buccleuch, and the farmers were mostly tenant farmers. Behind one of the fields was a small pond where we kids used to swim in the nude.

I remember vividly one time when, while the older people had dinner in the cottage, Fred and I stayed in the yard and sat on a little bench. They gave us our meal, which was half an egg each.

Fred looked at it in disgust. "Half an egg!"

"You got the best of it," I pointed out. "You got the bottom half, which is round and larger. I got the top, which is very pointed!"

Langside Cottage belonged to the Reid family. Mr. Reid was an official at a mine a few miles away. He and his wife had two sons, Tom and Jim, and a daughter, Alice, for whom they had built a special rose garden. They also had a vegetable garden. (The men of the family mostly kept to the horse yard, which was huge.)

Jim, the youngest child (and spoiled as a result), was a few years older than us. He was a card, always up to some mischief. He was done with lessons at the village school and did all the work around the cottage, looking after the horses and gardens, a big job.

Mother had arranged for us to live with the Reids while she returned to Edinburgh to work. She said she would come frequently to see us, which she did.

Sometimes Mother took us to Edinburgh to see Punch and Judy at Princes Street Gardens and to play on the lawns. One time, Mother took us to Leith, where we got on the boat and went under the Forth Bridge and as far as Rosyth. It must have been that trip, seeing the Forth Bridge, that made me decide to be an engineer: I wanted to build bridges and canals.

I was told that painting the bridge was a continuous process, that when they finished one end they started to paint again at the other. I could believe it, because it was such a huge structure.

The bridge over the Firth of Forth, ca. 1900 (Wikimedia Commons).

One Easter, Mother dyed eggs and took us to Arthur's Seat. At the time it had a lovely pond and lawns. (When I visited Arthur's seat during the First War, it was a terrible mess!)

When Mr. and Mrs. Reid went to Dalkeith or other nearby towns in their single-horse cart they would take Fred and me along and buy us treats: gingerbread cake, or a Lucky Bag (which contained a toy and miscellaneous candies), or a licorice strap, made of strips that we could peel apart and chew.

I remember one occasion when we were left at home under Jim's authority. Jim said, "Let us make some potato stovies." But we didn't have any potatoes, and of course, we couldn't use Mrs. Reid's spuds, or we would get found out. (You know what frugal Scots are like!)

Jim said, "Get out your little cart and get some out of the farmer's field next to the cottage."

The Scottish farmers in this district rotated their crops. The potatoes in this field had been harvested and were stored in the field. This was done by digging a huge ditch a couple of feet deep in the ground, lining it with straw, and then piling in the potatoes below and above the ground and covering them with straw sheaves.

Fred and I went out and filled our barrow with the potatoes, then I got up on the straw potato hut to see if anyone was coming before we went on the road home. The road had a little bend, and who should be coming along but the policeman from the village where our school was.

As it happened, I was pulling the cart. Fred spread himself out over it so the policeman wouldn't see the potatoes. We had a laugh with the policeman and then said goodbye when we pulled into the Reids' yard. We thought we'd pulled the wool over his eyes, but no doubt the policeman knew what we were up to!

Then Jim told us the Reids had been told to help themselves whenever they wanted turnips or potatoes, because they did favours for the farmer, such as acting as caretakers. This came as a great relief. Fred and I had thought we would go to prison for life, but it turned out it was just Jim delighting in giving us a scare.

Jim made the stovies, and they tasted lovely. We cleaned up everything so Mr. and Mrs. Reid would not know, but they were suspicious anyway, because the three of us couldn't eat our evening meal!

The Reids were great people. They understood the pranks of boys and closed their eyes to our little tricks. That being said, though, there was another time when Fred and I really *did* get into trouble.

We always went to a farm with a tin pitcher for the milk. When we came home from school, a walk of about three miles, sometimes we would have a drink out of the pitcher and put in water from the burn—but this time we drank too much and, of course, put in too much water.

Mrs. Reid remarked that the milk was getting too poor and looked at Fred and me; we looked guilty, and Mrs. Reid instantly knew what we had done. We were sent to bed without our supper. Jim sneaked in some food to us, but believe me, it was a lesson: we never took another drink of the milk.

In the morning, when we got up at seven to go to school, we would get a bowl of porridge, a slice of homemade bread, a glass of milk, and then away we went, meeting the farm children from the district as we walked the three and a half miles to our two-room school. In one room, a lady taught the juniors, while in the other, a man taught the higher grades.

For lunch, we'd have treacle on a slice of bread (we were given a penny each morning to pay for it) and a glass of water, and then away we'd go to play rounders or soccer (though, of course, in Scotland we called it football).

(Because I played rounders so much at school in Scotland, when I later became a junior baseball player in Toronto, I did not have to be told or taught the fundamentals of the game. They're the same: hit the ball and run to get on base. Of course, baseball is more scientific.)

In the afternoon, when we got home to the cottage, we were given a bowl of porridge until the men came home.

During our stay at Langside Cottage, an uncle, Mr. Andrew Baillie, who had married Mother's older sister and operated a steam laundry in the City of Toronto, visited his father in Edinburgh, and also visited my mother.

He acquainted her with the opportunities in Canada for her two boys, and after giving it a great deal of thought (because she held a very good position), Mother finally decided to emigrate to Canada when my uncle returned home.

It was the summer of 1902. I was nine and a half and my brother was seven and a half. At school, I had progressed to the senior grades, while Fred was still in the lower grades.

Mother came to Langside Cottage to take us back to Edinburgh. The Reids were downhearted to see us leave but wished us good luck in our new country of Canada.

We reached Edinburgh on the night of May 31, 1902—the day the Boer forces surrendered to end the Second Boer War—and stayed at a private hotel on Princes Street, with a balcony where we could sit and see Princes Street Gardens and Edinburgh Castle. The fireworks display was beyond description, and the people on the street were jubilant, shouting and dancing. The lady who operated the hotel and her daughter were with us, and we had a wonderful night.

The next morning came too soon. We departed Auld Reekie for Glasgow, where we saw the large ocean-going ships in the River Clyde, one of which was to take us to our new country: Canada.

What I could not understand about Glasgow was how the street cars operated with an overhead wire, because our cars in Edinburgh moved by gripping an underground cable (the same system used by the famous cable cars in San Francisco).

Springburn Road, Glasgow, ca. 1900 (from an old postcard).

I stood on the street trying to understand how the cars could move with a little wheel on the end of a pole, until someone informed me about the magic of electricity.

We boarded our ocean liner and were soon on our way down the Clyde. It was "Auld Lang Syne," at least for me.

2

A NEW COUNTRY

At the south end of Ireland we stopped to take on passengers from a ferry boat, then we were on our way across the Atlantic. It was a rough passage: several times the hatches were closed, preventing us from going on deck, and one time the angle of the deck was so acute my uncle's leg went through the deck guard railing.

We saw whales spouting water in the air, and fish following us. As we approached the shores, swarms of gulls surrounded the boat, looking for food.

We finally reached the St. Lawrence River, and then Quebec, where the third-class passengers disembarked. It was peculiar to see how the native French Quebec people dressed, and hear the language they used. We could not understand them. I wondered if I would have to learn a new language.

We finally got on a train (with very hard seats) and travelled through a beautiful countryside, seeing some wonderful sights. I immediately fell in love with my new country.

Yonge Street, Toronto, during the celebrations marking the end of the Boer War, just days before the Goodfellow family arrived (photo by William James, via Wikimedia Commons).

At last, we reached Toronto, where we were met by the Baillies: my mother's sister, Cecilia, four girls (Calia, Anna, Bella, and Alice), and a teenaged boy, William.

The transfer to a new country did not, at the beginning, work out very well, because it turned out that all my mother's relatives wanted from her was unpaid labour.

Fred and I attended Ryerson School. We wore Scottish clothes, and because we were immigrants we didn't get along with the teachers. As well, the children of our age and older would fight with us—if we could not outrun them, we had to stay and fight.

Fred, being younger, got a lot of beatings—I had to come to his aid many times, until we finally convinced them that we could hold our own, and better. (In fact, several times the fathers of some of the other children came to our house to complain about us giving their children black eyes and cut lips.)

As the weeks passed, it started getting cold. Mother asked for her pay and was told the keep for her and her two boys was the pay. "I work from seven in the morning until ten at night," she protested. "The boys need winter underwear and heavy clothes and I need clothes, too." It made no difference.

Finally, my aunt told my mother that her husband had paid our way to Canada.

Mother said, "That is a lie. I paid my own and the boys' fares."

Mrs. Baillie said, "Don't call my husband a liar."

Mother said, "Get him."

My uncle came in and admitted Mother was correct.

"What about the money you claimed you paid for the fare?" his wife demanded, and he admitted he had given the money to his father in Edinburgh.

After that, Mother left their home and got a temporary job.

W ithin a few months, Colonel George Taylor Denison III, who was police magistrate for the City of Toronto, asked Mother to be his housekeeper. Colonel Denison, an Empire Loyalist, had a big house and a large estate of land in the west end of Toronto.

Heydon Villa, George Taylor Denison III's estate (Toronto Star archives).

Mother accepted the position and was able to get us two boys a good boarding house near the colonel's home, where we could visit Mother. It was an ideal situation.

Time progressed, and we were growing up. Mother felt
we needed a parents' supervision. Colonel Denison owned a
house on Agnes Street (now Dundas), which he rented to
Mother at a very reduced rent. We attended Louisa Street
Public School.

*Louisa Street Public School, 1906. The school stood close to Holy Trinity
Church. The location was swallowed by the Eaton Centre (Toronto District
School Board Sesquicentennial Museum & Archives).*

Mother got a variety of jobs, so we were getting along
very well. Eventually, Mother decided Fred and I should
each learn a trade. I was mechanically inclined, while Fred
was interested in buildings.

A Mr. W. Blake (a nephew of Samuel Hume Blake, the

famous judge, philanthropist, and social reformer) got me an apprenticeship as a machinist with the A.R. Williams Machinery Co., where I served a four-year apprenticeship (which was to my liking), while also taking a four-year mechanical-drafting course at night.

When I finished my apprenticeship, in the summer of 1911, I decided to head out west, to Regina, Saskatchewan.

3

A MACHINIST IN REGINA

I could not get a job as a machinist in Regina at first, but did get a job as a helper at the Regina Foundry, building fire escapes (and erecting them, too). But one day, a job came into the shop that the machinist would not tackle.

The foreman, Mr. Bob Reid, said to me, "You are a machinist. Could you do the job?"

"Certainly," I said. It was a set-up faceplate job. I did it, and the customer was pleased. He came over and thanked me.

Mr. Reid talked to Mr. Cecil Springstein, the manager, telling him I should be rehired as a machinist and receive machinist pay. I was on the way up, receiving a higher hourly rate.

It was about this time that I decided I wanted to be a civil engineer. While repairing the city machinery, I met Mr. Roy

McCannell, a civil engineering student at Queen's University, who would go on to serve as City of Regina Engineer from 1914 until his retirement in 1955. Mr. McCannell was working with the city during his summer vacation, helping to lay the main city sewer on Seventh Avenue.

Downtown Regina, Saskatchewan, ca. 1911 (from an old postcard).

My shortcoming, I discovered, was that I did not have sufficient education—but I was lucky: two lawyers who had just graduated from the University of Toronto and Miss Marjorie Darrach undertook to prepare me, without remuneration, to study for my matriculation.

Mr. Andrew S. Sibbald and Arch Lamont McLean undertook to teach me algebra and geometry, but not trigonometry. Miss Darrach took on the job of teaching me French, German, and English composition. These subjects were required to enter the University of Toronto School of Practical Science. I progressed very well, but the practical side of physics, chemistry, and trigonometry were my downfall.

When I arrived in Regina, I joined the YMCA and entered into all types of sport. Jack White was the physical director and a Mr. Robinson was the secretary. They were both first-class men at their job.

I was boarding with Mr. and Mrs. Hirman Shaver (Mr. Shaver was a first-class mechanic, and had a woodworking shop in the yard behind his house), but I decided to leave there to take a room at the YMCA.

However, I was in the Shavers' home when the cyclone hit Regina on June 30, 1912. I watched it coming from the south and saw the houses on Cornwall Street tumbling down, one after the other. Mr. Shaver's home was blown off its foundation and the basement filled with water. (I rigged up a pump the next day and got rid of this water.)

Once the cyclone was over, I decided to wire my mother. I started up Cornwall Street, plowing through the mud, and on my way, people shouted at me, asking where I was going. I told them I was going to the telegraph station on Hamilton Street, next to the Alexander Hotel. Nearly everyone gave me a telegram to send, and the money to pay for it. I finally reached the station and handed in the telegrams. Fortunately, the money came out right!

Postcard Sam received after the Regina Cyclone, asking if he was all right.

It took a few days to get straightened around, then I went back to work.

Aftermath of the Regina Cyclone, June 30, 1912 (Archives Canada).

I had played junior baseball with the Diamonds in Toronto, and when I came to Regina, I played on the YMCA team. I also did a little running and was in the Saskatchewan Olympics Trials. There were Alvin Hammond, Stewart Hasting, and myself in the sprints: the 100, the 220, and the 440. The only one who made it to Winnipeg was Hammond, but his time was not good enough, so he came home.

In the fall of 1912, I joined the Regina Rugby Club (which eventually became the Saskatchewan Roughriders) as a substitute flying wing. (The flying wing was a chap named Dale, and he was good.) Later, while attending Toronto Technical School, I was asked to join the Toronto Argonauts, but declined and played for the school team instead.

I decided to leave Regina in October 1913 to try to enroll at Toronto Technical School, where I had taken my four-year course in mechanical drafting and mathematics. (They called it mensuration, dealing with calculation in mechanical drafting.)

4

EDUCATION AND ENLISTMENT

I was interviewed by the assistant principal for day schools, Mr. J.M. Warren. After a casual examination, he told me to enroll in the fourth year, which taught ten junior subjects and three senior: senior algebra, geometry, and an extra, analytical geometry and trigonometry. Since I hadn't taken trigonometry, one of the mathematics teachers, Dr. W.H. Rutherford, took an interest in me and gave me special lessons after school. I soon caught up with the rest of the class. (Interestingly, Mr. Warren and Dr. Rutherford would later author a book together, entitled *Mathematics for Technical Schools*.)

My class at Toronto Technical School had only twenty-five students. We sat for our matriculation in the summer of 1914. In algebra, we had only gone as far as permutations, combinations, and the binomial theorem, and when we got the algebra examination paper, there were questions we could not answer (although we tried our best).

Toronto Technical School, 1908 (from an old postcard).

Mr. Warren came into our examination room, saw us with long faces, and asked what the problem was. He looked at the examination paper and frowned. "Something's wrong," he said. "Some of these questions are not on your curriculum."

For the moment, that was that.

That summer, I got a job on the new Welland Ship Canal, working for Dominion Bridge as a machinist. After that, I was even more taken with the idea of being a civil engineer.

All of us who had written our matriculation in 1914 returned to school in 1915. We were informed we had written the University of Toronto's first-year engineering students' examination paper, while they had received *our* examination paper. We had all received better than a sixty-percent average overall, but we had only gotten a thirty-nine in algebra, whereas forty was a pass.

Dr. A.C. MacKay, our principal, took the matter up the with the department of education, and it was agreed that we had all passed in mathematics. Mr. Warren informed us that, as a result, we did not have to attend school: we were free to go and enlist in the services if we wished.

We had a meeting outside on the steps of the school to talk over what unit it would be best for us engineering students to enlist in. One of the students told us that the Third Divisional Ammunition Column and the Third Divisional Supply Column were wanting ambulance drivers, motorcycle dispatch riders, and truck drivers. Both were having a difficult time getting qualified personnel, so the students thought either would be okay to join.

The students appointed me to go and have an interview with the adjutants of the two units, which I did. The adjutants were delighted when I informed them that there were approximately twenty of us and told me of the requirements for us to get into either one of the units: we had to pass a mechanical-knowledge examination and a driving test.

We had another meeting of the students who had not yet enlisted. (Some of them, through the influence of their parents, had received commissions in different units, leaving about eighteen of us.) I explained what had taken place at the meeting and told them about the mechanical and driving tests. They all agreed they could pass the tests, but they suggested I enlist first, which I did.

This took place on a Friday. I went to the adjutant of the Third Divisional Supply Column, who interviewed me, and then set my test for Monday. Then I went over to the T. Eaton Co. store and purchased a book on the theory of the automobile, which I studied Saturday and Sunday.

I sat for the verbal examination and did so well they had to work not to give me 100 percent. They kept crossing me until I made a slip in the number of thousandths-of-an-inch gap needed in the distributor and spark plugs. I gave them the wrong answer and then corrected myself, but they would not allow it and gave me ninety-one percent.

The truth was, I knew more about an automobile than the individual who examined me (he was looking at a question-and-answer list). He told me to wait while he went and talked to the adjutant. They had a long conversation, then returned to interview me.

They wanted the particulars of my knowledge, and I just told them I was a matriculation student from Toronto Technical School, studying to go to the Toronto School of Practical Science, to study to be a civil engineer. I did not tell them I was a machinist and a mechanical draftsman, because then they would have had me sent to the engineering units, which were short of these professions, and I would have been kept in Canada. I wanted to go overseas.

They informed me that if I enlisted they would make me a lance corporal, and later a sergeant, but that for the present I would be the Automobile Mechanical Examiner. I agreed and enlisted at that meeting.

Sam in his army uniform.

I then told the rest of the students what had taken place and to come down on Tuesday, which they did. I passed them all: some joined the Third Divisional Supply Column and some the Ammunition Column. The Supply Column wanted 400 drivers and 200 loaders. The Ammunition Column required 200 motor drivers and 200 loaders.

I was also the first of our group to take a driving test. I passed, but was admonished to not be such a fast driver.

We did all types of drilling. For rainy days, the government had rented a hall in Elm Street Methodist Church between Terauley (now Bay) Street and Yonge Street, where we did boxing, wrestling, indoor racing, etc.

I was in my element. I had joined the Toronto West End YMCA while I was apprenticing, and had boxed Oscar "Battling" Nelson, Ad "Michigan Wildcat" Wolgast, and Joe "Old Master" Gans (each of whom had been lightweight champion of the world), plus other Americans, at the Labour Temple on Church Street when they were wanting a workout before appearing on the stage at the Star Theatre or the Gaiety Theatre (Toronto's two burlesque houses). Most likely, they pulled their punches, but I used to feel that I held my own. I certainly learned a lot.

Some of the boxers' managers even called on my mother, to get her consent for me to go to New York to train as a boxer, but Mother said, "No, I don't want my boy to have a broken nose or cauliflower ears."

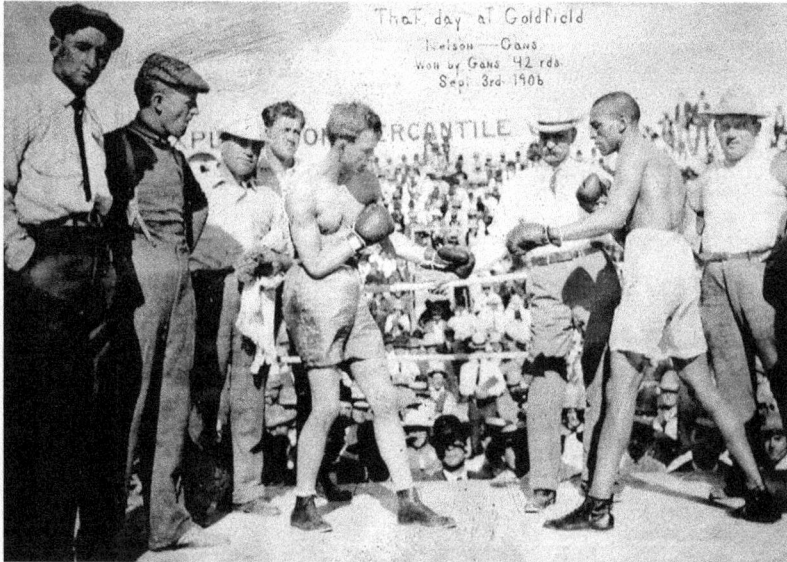

Two boxers with whom Sam sparred, Oscar "Battling" Nelson (left) and Joe "Old Master" Gans (right), before their "Fight of the Century" at Goldfield, Nevada, Labor Day, 1906 (via The Boxing Magazine.com).

After that, she admonished me not to run away. I said, "I won't."

We stayed around Toronto until we were ready to go overseas, finally leaving the city on Wednesday, April 19, 1916.

5

FAREWELL TO FAMILY

Mother came to the station with her friends to see me on my way. She had had a difficult time recently. First, she had fallen on the sidewalk in front of a butcher shop on Bloor Street—the fool of a butcher had thrown sawdust on the slippery ice—and dislocated her hip. She was taken to the Western Hospital, where she also had to have an appendicitis operation.

Since I was the corporal in charge of the first coach, when the order was given to board the passenger train, I ordered the men to hurry and get on, then went to my mother to kiss her good-bye. She looked at me sadly and said, "Sam, I will never see you again."

"Yes, you will, Mother," I said. "I'll come back!"

She nodded. "Yes, you will come back...but I won't be here."

Mother, a very religious Presbyterian, always seemed to have great insight and foresight. I remembered well that during the First Battle of Ypres, Mother said to me, "Something has happened to Jimmy. He is dead."

"Jimmy" was James Martin, my mother's favourite nephew. After his father, also named James, a Liverpool police inspector, was killed in a riot, Alice, his mother, my mother's sister, came to Canada with four children. Being from that type of a family, the two boys, John and Joseph, enlisted in the first contingent of the Princess Patricia's Canadian Light Infantry.

What Mother said about Jimmy's fate was absolutely true: in later years, I read his name on the Menin Gate Memorial to the Missing. (His brother, Joseph, was also killed in France, in 1917.) So, when Mother told me she wouldn't be there when I came home, it was chilling. I had no time to think about it, though: I had to board the train with the others.

We left the station at 11:40 p.m., travelled east, and at 9:30 a.m. reached Montreal, where we were inspected by a brigadier general. After that came a route march through the city. We left Montreal at 2 p.m.

When we got back on the train I said to myself, *This is a great country we are passing through.* All the men in my coach were very happy. Where they got the "liquid" I didn't know. As long as they behaved themselves it suited me.

I got up early and was hard at it all day, placed on duty as usual. *They must think I am an iron man or perpetual-motion machine*, I remember thinking. I was then put on guard again all night. I had three-quarters of an hour's sleep every two hours.

We were aboard a troop train that also carried other units, such as the Strathcona Horse and Sixty-Third Battalion. While I was on duty, it came to my ears that there were several cases of spinal meningitis on the train, but when we reached St. John's (at 10 p.m. on Friday, April 21, 1916), no one had gotten sick in my carriage. (Well, some had a big head from overindulgence, but they got over it after they got some food in their stomach.)

On Saturday, April 22, 1916, reveille was at 4 a.m. I was on duty as orderly corporal, and got three meals for the boys. We boarded the Canadian Pacific liner *Metagama*. The Sixty-Third Battalion was left on the wharf because so many of its members were infected with spinal meningitis and were waiting for medical attention. After a while, they found an empty shed and slept there, waiting for doctors.

I asked my section lieutenant to relieve me of my stripe, but no luck, so the next day I was up at 6 a.m., had breakfast, and paraded my guard to the hurricane deck on the port side to have them inspected. The men from other companies got the devil but mine didn't.

The Canadian Pacific liner Metagama.

We left St. John's at 5:15 p.m. and sailed out into the Atlantic Ocean. Lights-out was at 9 p.m., and we anchored at Halifax at 4:20 a.m. Also in the bay were the *Olympic*, *Lapland,* and *Empress of Britain*. The gossip was that we were to be there until the 28th. The *Empress of Britain,* an 18,000-ton boat, had 4,500 troops on board, while the *Metagama*, a 13,000-ton boat, had 1,700 troops. Aboard the *Metagama*, the boys named their passageways Yonge Street and Hogan's Alley, with Lizzie Lane quite near.

While we waited, I was appointed fire corporal for the Third Divisional Supply Column. We had a trial maneuver.

In case of fire on the ship, I had to run as fast as I could to the bridge, to the senior lieutenant colonel and to the captain of the ship. They then gave me a written order to take to Major Mayall, who explained my duties.

After I left him, I began to think that I was going to be like the captain; if we were torpedoed I would have to go down with the ship. "I guess my life is not worth a tinker's damn," I muttered.

The gossip was wrong: we left Halifax on Wednesday, August 26, at 4 p.m., heading into a very rough ocean. The boat rocked from side to side and the bow plunged until the water buried the forward deck.

Of course, we were all seasick.

I was placed on the athletic committee that Sergeant Hamilton was heading to organize different sports for the troops.

The men were late for the 2 p.m. parade and had to do fatigue the following day; I was the ship's corporal for that night, because it was our Divisional Supply Column guard. I picked out thirty-six men and they certainly kicked.

One day a soldier of the Sixty-Third Infantry Battalion asked if he could box me. He weighed 240 pounds, while I was only a lightweight, 135 pounds. I said, "No chance!", thinking that if he ever hit me he would knock me into the ocean.

But then everyone started making remarks that got under my skin. Even though I knew it was a put-up job, I said, "Okay, I will box him."

I think everyone on the ship turned out to see me get beat up! It was to be three rounds. We put on the gloves and the referee gave the signal to start.

He made a lunge at me, but I jumped out of the way. Then I gave him a good punch on the chin. He shook his head and went at me again. I smashed him on the nose, and he started bleeding. This went on for all the first round.

Soldiers watching a boxing match on board a New Zealand troopship during the First World War. (Photo by Ian Kidman, from Alexander Turnbull Library, Ref: 1/4-027515-F.)

His second gave him instructions for the second round. I moved backwards, and he chased me all over the ring. Every time he lunged at me, I wasn't there. I gave him black eyes, so he could hardly see, and the referee stopped the fight.

Then who wanted a go at me but a loader in our outfit

who was a Hamilton Tigers rugby player. I said, "Okay." We only went two rounds, then again, the referee stopped the fight.

We went below together. He asked me why I had to hit him so hard and I asked him why he hit me so hard. The skin from the roof of my mouth was lying on my tongue!

That pleased him. He did not like me because I had turned him down as a driver on account of his not having any mechanical knowledge, so for him, it was a grudge fight.

Much later, in France, after we had taken Vimy Ridge, some of us had a day to ourselves and decided to go swimming in the Scarpe River, near Arras. The banks were high, so those of us who could swim ran along the bank and dove into the water.

The first chap who had boxed me did the same thing, but he could not swim, and started to drown. I was afraid to go after him because he was so strong, but I went down the bank to the water. There I saw a root of a tree was sticking out like a rope, so I grabbed it and went into the water. The drowning man grabbed my ankle and I pulled him out.

Then I asked him why he jumped in when he could not swim. He said if I could do it, he wanted to do the same!

We had church parade on Sunday, April 30, and the chaplain of the Sixty-Third Infantry Battalion preached a good sermon. By then we were in a dangerous section of the ocean. The warship had left us, but our convoy was joined by four torpedo boats, wonderful boats that could turn on their own length, and so swift they could circle the convoy in a few minutes.

British coastal torpedo boat (Imperial War Museum).

They stayed with us while we were rerouted to north of Ireland, between Ireland and Scotland, and then to Liverpool. I saw lots of places I had read about in Sir Walter Scott's books.

6

NOT-SO-JOLLY OLD ENGLAND

W e were up at 4:30 a.m. on May 4, 1916 and reached Liverpool soon after. (As we disembarked I had a look inside one of the torpedo boats—they were all engine.) We immediately got on the train, but didn't leave Liverpool until 11:30 a.m. We passed Crewe, Rugby, and the outskirts of London, and reached Shorncliffe, Kent, at 5:15 p.m. From the train, we marched to Napier Barrack, where we went under canvas.

What a place! Its nickname was Peckerhill, because this was the place where they isolated all the troops who had venereal disease before they were sent to Cambridge Hospital. We lost a number of our own troop after our inspection. Then the place was disinfected for us.

It was near the north entrance to Shorncliffe Army Camp, which included St. Martin's Plain Camp (to the west of the main camp), Moore Barracks, Napier Barracks, Risborough Barracks, Ross Barracks, and Somerset Barracks. To one side was a hill so steep you had a difficult time climbing it; there was a row of houses at the bottom, and on the other side was a road leading into the camp.

A view of a portion of Shorncliffe Army Camp (WartimeCanada.ca).

The cookhouse was situated near this steep incline and played a part in something that took place at a later date (which I will explain presently).

We were informed by our officers that we were to get new officers. We would be broken up and go as a draft to the six units already in France: the First, Second, and Third Supply Columns and the First, Second, and Third Ammunition Columns.

I was reappointed a lance corporal, the lowest of the noncommissioned officers (NCOs) and the workhorse of the unit. I was corporal of the guard many times; we had four points to mount guard and I did them all one after the other, while other NCOs did nothing but walk around showing their stripes.

I pointed out to Regimental Sergeant Major Wilcox that it was against military law and King's regulations. All he did was pat me on the back and say he would look into the matter. Then Company Sergeant Major Bourne took the question into his hands, and I was corporal of the guard every other night. I also did a number of other jobs around the camp when they required a NCO.

The company sergeant major was an old fusilier who had served time in the army at many different places in the British Empire. He told me they were going to make me corporal of the guard on the truck depot outside the camp. He then said, "When Sergeant Allan tells you that you are on guard duty, tell him you won't go on guard."

I said, "I can't do that, I will be put in the clink."

He replied, "Do what I tell you, and don't tell anyone you were talking to me."

I said, "Will I come out of this okay?"

He said, "Yes."

Sure enough, Sergeant Allan came up to me that afternoon and said, "You are corporal of the guard at the truck depot."

I said, "I am not, because I have been on guard every night and on corporal duty through the day."

He said, "Will you come with me and tell Regimental Sergeant Major Wilcox what you have said to me?"

I said, "Yes."

We went to see the sergeant major and Sergeant Allan told him what I had said.

He said, "Do you mean it?"

I said, "Yes."

He said, "You know what it means, disobeying an order during a war?"

I said, "Yes."

He said, "Be a good boy and go on guard," and dismissed me.

Instead I went to my tent, put on my best clothes, and went to Shorncliffe, returning to camp at 11 p.m. They were all waiting for me and I was immediately put under arrest.

The next day I was supposed to go to the officers' orderly room, but instead they put me in front of Regimental Sergeant Major Harris, the head NCO of Napier Barracks. He gave me a terrible dressing-down, and all types of dirty jobs to do for several days.

One day, Company Sergeant Bourne saw me. He thought the punishment had gone far enough, so he told me to demand to go to the colonel's orderly room, which I did.

Sergeant Major Harris was taken aback. "Who has been talking to you and giving you advice?" he said.

I just told him that the guard duties I had been doing were against King's rules and regulations. He knew he was beaten. He dismissed me, sent me back to my unit, and told me to be a good boy.

I was made corporal of the camp guard that night. Sergeant Allan was having another go at me.

During the night, our officers, along with some of our senior NCOs, had lots of liquor flowing in one of the tents on my territory. The guard I had posted notified me they were making noise and running around outside the tent. He tried to get them to quiet down, but they just laughed at him.

I went up to the tent. They stopped for a while, but then it got worse. I went back again, and a lieutenant (I won't mention his name, but I will never forget it) came out and aimed his revolver at me. I ran away from the tent, with him following me, revolver pointed at me.

I finally lost him. Then I went back to the party tent and told the officers that I was going to put the lieutenant in the guard tent on charges of drunkenness and disobedience. The officers found him very quickly and took the revolver away from him, and I went back to the guard to tell him everything was okay.

My company officer came to the guard tent and said, "Goodfellow, forget it."

I said, "Very well, sir," but then I told him to stop the party at once; which he did.

The next day some of the officers came to me and

thanked me. I had had enough common sense to hush the matter up. When I eventually took an officers' course, the lecturer said, "Know what to see and what not to see." (I will give you an example later on.)

On Thursday, May 25, there was a small revolution. We lined up for dinner; I was eighth in line and the sergeant-cook put a lump of fat, a small potato, and some grease in my dixie. I looked at it, then looked at him.

He said, "Go on, that's all you are going to get."

The troops before me and the ones following got the same junk. They were wild about it, and since I was the senior there, they asked what I was going to do about it.

I said, "I am going to Folkestone to buy my meal."

They said, "You are going to see RSM Wilcox."

I said, "Very well."

I went to the regimental sergeant major's tent and showed him my dinner. A number of the troops were behind me. He just said, "Well, you had better eat it."

The boys started shouting. I left and went to my tent to get ready to go to Folkestone.

All hell broke loose then. They grabbed the permanent cookhouse gang, beat them up, tore down the cookhouse and storage sheds, and raised the very devil.

While this was going on, word got out to headquarters, and down came the colonel and troops on horseback. They tried to stop the riot but could not. The boys started shouting, "Where is Corporal Goodfellow?"

I heard them in my tent, but I did not know what to do. Wearing my baseball sweater (blue body with white trim and a big green maple leaf on the front), I stepped out.

The colonel shouted to me. I went up to him and saluted. He said, "You started this."

I told him, "I did not."

He said, "Can you stop them?"

I said, "Yes." I shouted at them, "Fall in by company," which they did. I lined them up like we did on parade and turned them over to the colonel.

He said, "Put them at ease," and then had his adjutant read the riot act.

The men got uneasy and I thought the riot would break out again. I shouted at them, "Silence!"

The colonel, after hearing their complaint and inspecting some of the dixies containing the food, said he would send down food from headquarters. He told me to pick out eight men, including myself, and march to his orderly room. We had four companies, so I picked out two men from each company. Then I told the troops to behave themselves and dismissed them.

The eight of us marched to headquarters: on the way we met the new food going to our boys.

In the orderly room, the colonel again blamed me for the uprising, and I again denied it. Finally, he calmed down and asked us how long we had been getting such terrible meals.

We then told him the cooking staff were selling our food for what they could get at the row of houses down the hill behind the cookhouse. We also told him that women with baby carriages were going out of the camp with food, with their babies sitting on it.

He gave the eight of us a good dressing-down—but he also thanked us for the information and had the matter investigated. After that, there were no more baby carriages going through the camp. We also had a new cookhouse gang —I never saw our other cooks again.

I have not mentioned anything about our physical training; well, we had plenty. Our officers knew we would be in competition with other units when we got to England, which was correct, and so before we left Canada, the troops that were athletically inclined were singled out and given training at the Toronto Central YMCA.

The building had two gymnasiums, with a big door between. For a thirty-five-yard race the door would be opened, so you started in one gym and finished in the other.

On Thursday, March 9, 1916, we had what they called "The Assault-At-Arms." I won my heat in the thirty-five-yard dash in four seconds and won the final in four and two-fifths seconds.

In the relay race, Sergeant Hogarth fell, but the rest of the team (Gordon Huckle, Delmore, Sergeant Hamilton, and me) made up the time and won the race. Later, Warrant Staff Officer Hogarth and Staff Sergeant Hamilton were rugby players for the Toronto Argonauts. (As I mentioned earlier, before I joined up, I was asked to come to the Argonaut practice for tryout at flying wing, but I refused—I didn't want to take a chance on being hurt while I was working my way through technical school.)

Soldiers line up for baths at the Toronto Central YMCA in 1915 (Pringle & Booth, Toronto Star Archives).

We had another athletic meet in Toronto; our unit, the Third Divisional Supply Column, against the Third Divisional Ammunition Column. We won in points, 48 to 44.

We had other little contests on the ship, and Sergeant Hamilton put me on his committee to help with the sports. They were a great success and kept the troops interested. Our CO (commanding officer), Major Mayall, was well-pleased.

We did no more serious athletic training until we got to our camp at Shorncliffe. There, on Victoria Day, May 24,

1916, we had a Third Divisional Supply and Ammunition Column athletic meet on Sir John Moore Plains. I won my heat in the 100 yards, and then won the final. I was disqualified in the potato race because I had knocked down the stand. I came second in the NCO race, but our relay team, Hogarth, Carmichael, Hamilton, and Goodfellow, won the relay. I also won the 100-yard low hurdles and the running broad jump.

The cigarette case Sam won in athletic competition at Shorncliffe Army Camp. It reads, "Won by Lce. Corp. S.J. Goodfellow, N.C.O. 100 yd dash, C.A.S.C. Games, May 24, 1916, Shorncliffe Camp."

The CO of the camp was at the event and gave out the prizes. I was up several times to get my prize. Finally, he said, "Goodfellow again! Who the hell are you?" I just laughed and said nothing. I gave all my prizes away except a cigarette case and a set of two brushes in a leather case.

We also had an athletic meet of the Canadian forces at Cheriton Cricket Field. I won my heat and placed in the final. After that, I was picked to be on the team to represent Canada in the 100-, 220-, and 440-yard races, and the relay race, in an athletic competition of all the British forces, to be held in London. We went on special training under a sergeant major from an Edmonton unit. He was a mess and didn't know anything about training athletes. I did fairly well at the first, but so overtrained that I could not run and was left at camp.

However, I still appeared in the program, which Gordon Murray showed me. I was listed in a handicap event, with a five-yard handicap on Fred Appleby, an English runner who was champion of the world in the 100- and 220-yard events.

Haliburton, from Edmonton, was the best of the Canadians and went to London but did not place. The only event the Canadians won was the obstacle race: that was won by Gordon Murray of our unit. He got the Lord French Silver Tray; a beautiful prize.

A fter the training, I returned to my unit and was made corporal of the guard again. I heard very soon that the company sergeant major had been reduced in rank and had left our unit. He was the only real soldier among us.

I waited for an opportunity to get posted to another job. Finally, word came that they wanted an NCO for office duty, and I got the job. It suited me fine. I could sleep in the office at night by clearing off the table, wrapping myself in a blanket, and stretching out. I had an alarm to wake me just before reveille. Then I got washed, had breakfast, and was ready for work.

A draft of truck drivers was made up to augment the division's supply and ammunition columns in France. When I got the office job, I took off my lance-corporal stripe so that if a draft was going to France, I would be on it.

Lieutenant Brouse had just returned from France, so I knew what was required for the First, Second, and Third Truck Columns. We were going over the list of drivers who had come from Canada. He came across the name Corporal Goodfellow, and said, "Who the devil is he? I have never met him." I said nothing until he said, "Is that you?" and I had to admit it.

Then he said, "Where is your stripe?"

I told him I had removed it when I got that job so I would be on the first draft for France.

He said, "You attach it, or I will take you to the orderly room for misbehaviour!"

"But, sir," I said, "if I put it on, my chances to go to France with this draft will be nil."

He laughed. "You really want to go."

I begged him to allow me to put my name on the draft, and finally he said, "Okay, place your name on the list, but I will certainly miss you, since you know everything about the camp!"

I thanked him most sincerely.

I was the only one of the original Third NCOs to go to France. During my time with the drivers of all the divisions, I did not see any of our former NCOs. They all had good jobs at the depot.

7

LE HAVRE TO THE SOMME

We left for France on Sunday, September 24, 1916. We marched down with full equipment to Shorncliffe Railway Station at 9 a.m., changed trains at Redhill, and reached Southampton at 2:30 p.m.

We departed from the dock at 10 p.m. for Le Havre. We were at semi-attention on the main deck all night. I found a wonderful corner and went to sleep—the submarines didn't worry me.

We reached Le Havre at 5 a.m., had a breakfast of our twenty-four-hour emergency rations (bully beef and hard tack), then got off the boat at 8:30 a.m., only to discover the military at Le Havre did not know what to do with us: they had not been notified of our draft coming!

When all our papers were checked by our officer and the

officers at the port, it was found that we had disembarked at the wrong place. We should have gone to Rouen.

Postcard of Le Havre in 1917 (State Library of Western Australia).

We marched to the army service barracks, but they had no room for us, so we marched through the town of Le Havre and through the woods to the Canadian rest camp. Again, they had no room for us, so we marched to a valley where they had built a pier on wooden bridgework, with a pavilion at the end. Our officers told us to stay there for the night. I found a nice place under the structure, wrapped myself in my blanket, and went to sleep.

Reveille was blown at 4:30 a.m. but we only got up in time for a breakfast of bread, cheese, and a mug of tea. It tasted like cake after eating bully beef and hard tack!

Roll call was at 8:45 a.m., then we were dismissed to loaf around until noon, when we had bare bread and another mug of tea for dinner. We continued sitting and walking around until 6:30 p.m., when we marched seven miles to the station at Le Havre.

This journey was the worst of my career. We had to go down a medium incline. The street had no sewerage, so waste matter was carried away by a gutter on each side of the street.

It is a peculiar thing: the inhabitants of this part of France have not forgotten their hatred of the British for the burning at the stake of Jeanne d'Arc. They showed their resentment of us by throwing their swill of the previous night at us. We had to jump and duck from side to side to miss their body rubbish. I was lucky, jumping to the other side of the street, but some of the troops got a sprinkling.

We marched through the main parts of the city of Le Havre to the station, where we were assigned to French third-class carriages, which are like the British type, with passengers sitting opposite one another, but on wooden seats.

The Imperial troops returning from leave and going to the front at the Somme got a meal, but there was no food for us. We purchased cake from French civilians selling it at the station. We departed for Rouen at 1:30 a.m.

Two of our men slept on the floor between the seats. I tried to sleep sitting up, but it was impossible on the hard wooden seats. It was a terrible night, so I was glad when we reached Rouen at 5:30 a.m.

146 ROUEN. — La Statue de Jeanne d'Arc — LL.

Statue of St. Jeanne d'Arc in Rouen (from an old postcard).

We were marched to a barrack outside of Rouen and saw some wonderful sights of the place, such as the monument to St. Jeanne d'Arc (1412-1430), the Maid of Orleans, the French national heroine, martyred by being burned at the stake. (Today we, with our new line of thought on life, consider this a dreadful mistake on the part of the British.) We also saw a great drawbridge over the dirty, filthy Seine.

Again, there was no place for us, because they had not been notified about our draft. After a meal and roll call, etc., we were dismissed. I was lucky: I found a two-wheel French cart full of straw, with the shafts resting on the ground. I curled up in the straw and had a wonderful afternoon snooze, but what a cleaning-up job I had afterwards! (I always blessed the medical profession for our inoculations; otherwise, we soldiers would have been dead ducks from what we had to go through.)

A place was found to quarter us for a few days. An ex-Toronto policeman in our group informed the sergeant major that I was an engineer and draftsman. I was then paraded before the CO of the barracks. I denied it: I told him I was a technical-school student, because I did not want to stay behind the lines at a base.

The drafts personnel were made up before we left Rouen Depot. I was placed in the group for the Third Divisional Supply Column, which suited me.

We left Rouen on Wednesday, October 4, 1916, at 4 p.m. for the Somme, departing on a cattle car, suitable for carrying thirty *homme* or eight *cheval*. We did not get an evening meal, so all we did was roll ourselves in our blankets and go to sleep after chewing some hard tack.

When we finally awakened, we were nearing Abbeville. It was a beautiful part of France, a country worth fighting for.

Abbeville had a lovely large cathedral, but a shell or bomb had been dropped on the spire and the Virgin Mary's figure had been knocked from its position. This was the town where the first tank arrived for the Somme.

When we reached Val de Maison, we were informed where we were to report for duty; eighteen drivers to the Third Divisional Ammunition Column and ten to the Supply Column.

Our Third Divisional Supply Column was located at Rubempré. We started out, and did it rain! We were soaked, but had to walk, carrying our kit bags, rifles, etc. We stopped at a concentration camp for the night. We went to a tent that had a floor of mud. Being dead tired, I put down my rubber sheet, wrapped my blanket around me, and went to sleep. In the morning my body form was baked in the mud.

I got something to eat and started to look for the column. I finally found it and was put on duty as a second driver on a Locomobile four-ton truck with a coloured chap named Senior, a Jamaican, who had been transferred from the Second Division.

We were then ordered to go to Achieux, which was the railhead, to get a load of bully beef, etc. The engagement of

Flers-Courcelette at the Somme River was on. It was the Battle of the Somme.

The traffic was terrible, but Senior wanted me to get the feel of the truck. It was in terrible shape: poor clutch, poor foot brake, and no emergency brake. It certainly needed repairs.

The position among commercial vehicles occupied by the Riker Truck is due to the quality of service it delivers, whether to manufacturers, or to the Nations.

High service-quality is never an accident. The Riker Worm Drive Truck is engineered and built by The Locomobile Company of America.

Delivery of three and four ton sizes is available to those to whom continuous and economical service is of prime consequence.

RIKER   Built by THE LOCOMOBILE COMPANY OF AMERICA
BRIDGEPORT,   CONNECTICUT
Send For Book, "RIKER TRUCKS IN ACTION"

First World War-vintage advertisement for Locomobile trucks, like the one Sam first drove in France.

Next day, I drove again in column for Achieux, and *bang!*

I got it. One of the trucks in a column coming towards us broke a steering column and ran into the second truck ahead of me, smashing him. The truck in front, a Pierce-Arrow, saw it and stopped dead. I ran into him, smashing my radiator and two headlights.

After towing the two damaged trucks back to our park, I said to myself, "Now I will get it!", but not a word was said. The officers knew what shape all our trucks were in.

They didn't have a Loco radiator but had a spare Pierce-Arrow radiator. The officer asked me if I could make it work, and after looking at the top and bottom connections, I said, "Yes." I asked the officer if I could repair the clutch and brakes.

"Can you do it?"

I said, "Yes."

When I was through repairing that old truck, it was okay.

I was then put on as spare driver in our section. I went out every day, by myself, on a different truck, reported to the officer the faults of the vehicle, and then repaired it. This went on while we were on the Somme front, but then we got orders to move north. We all got new Daimler Knight trucks, which were lovely vehicles. I was still a spare driver.

When we moved north, the company captain chose me as a lead truck driver. He and the sergeant-major sat in front with me, with the map in front of them.

8

A BAD WINTER

On the way north, I began to realize why I had been chosen to drive the lead truck. I had taken matriculation French and German in high school and could make myself understood by and get information from the natives, if they didn't go too fast. I would put in an English word when I didn't know the French word and got on just fine. The officer said to the sergeant major, "I guess I made a good choice when I chose Goodfellow as the lead driver!"

(I learned later that he was engaged to the sister of the girl that I chummed with at Tech. Her father was chief of police for the City of Toronto. I gave her my form pin, which now I often wish I still had!)

A peculiar thing happened on the way north. We met an infantry battalion. When we got to the head of the column, our officer made me stop. He asked the young lieutenant where he was going. The lieutenant said to Warloy-Baillon, which was near the Eighth Reserve camp on the Varennes road.

Our officer said we are going there, too, and added, "I have a number of empty trucks that could give you all a ride."

The young officer said, "We are a Scottish regiment. They are going to walk every foot of the way."

They were mentally and physically exhausted. They had just come out of the trench at the Somme.

My officer said, "Very well," and told me to start. The lieutenant told his sergeant major to give orders to march. The sergeant major looked around. I am certain he saw that some of his troops were climbing into the empty trucks, but even though he knew what was happening, all he did was give the order to march. I started slowly, to give the balance of the troops time to jump into our trucks, which they did.

When we got to our destination, they all got out of our trucks. I am certain the Scottish officer did not have many men to lead. The young lieutenant, in my opinion, had just received his commission and had not been in the trenches, or he would have had sympathy for his men.

We finally reached Saint-Pol, which was on the outskirts of our territory, and then reached Aubigny, which was our railhead, and parked at Tilloy-lès-Mofflaines, which was our headquarters for three months before the start of the Battle of Vimy Ridge.

We then moved to Olhain, which was our headquarters for the battle, and did we work! Out on the road at 5 and 6 a.m., and back at 10 and 11 p.m. Being on the spare board, I never got a day off. When someone was sick, I took his truck and his orders.

The winter of 1916 was a terrible winter. We were lucky we had a Saurer truck in our column. Nearly all the rest at that time were Daimler sleeve-valve types, which would not start in the morning. The old Saurer would start if you looked at it!

A 1916-model Saurer truck.

The Saurer would pull one Daimler to get it started. Then we would have two trucks. These would start two more, and so on, and so on, until we had all the trucks moving. Some of the Daimler trucks had a pocket in the head that would not drain when we drained the engines, so the heads would crack. New heads were rushed to us and we changed them very quickly. Later we got antifreeze and stopped draining the engines.

One day, when we were short of trucks, Senior took the Thornycroft automobile and I took the Saurer to Aubigny for goods. While Senior was cranking his car, he broke his wrist. I took him to the hospital and then he was sent to Blighty.

I was always the willing horse, and sure enough, I got double fatigue and bronchitis.

An eighteen-pound artillery regiment had arrived from India and was stationed in our village of Olhain. They had a medical officer, so I dragged myself over to him, but all I got was a calling down for not being washed and smart like the artillery soldiers. I told him that if I could dress like them I would not come to see him.

He gave me a pink pill, which did no good. The next day, I went back again and got another calling down and another coloured pill. The next day, I dragged myself over again and got a calling down *again*, and another coloured pill. The fourth time I thought I was going to die, and went over to him practically on my hands and knees. As I was crossing the street, Michael, our Quebecois sergeant, shouted at me to go out on a Daimler truck alone. I looked at him through my bleary eyes and got in the truck with the orders.

All that day, officers would come up to me and tell me I was sick.

I drove to our park, got out of the truck, and collapsed. The no-good corporal passed by and I said to him, "Take me to the OC (officer in charge)."

He said, "You're going to the hospital."

They got me an ambulance and away I went. By this time, I was vomiting blood. The doctor at the advanced hospital was on duty and he looked after me. He was a young doctor from Winnipeg. Within a week he came and interviewed me and I told him the whole story.

He said, "The devil, they can't do that to our boys!"

The accommodation in the hospital was of the roughest. It was a large tent with little wooden horses six inches high, with straw kits and blankets top and bottom. There was very little male help.

On one side of me was a Salvation Army soldier, and all I got from him was, "Are you saved?"

On the other side was an automobile racing driver. All he talked about was his racing against Barney Oldfield. But he did me a favour—he told the Sally to shut up and let the youngster have some peace.

The doctor, on one of his rounds, said, "Goodfellow, I am going to keep you here for a month. You need a rest and you're going to get it.

I progressed very rapidly, and one day the doctor came to

me and said, "I will let you go now. You are okay, and I am being transferred to a large hospital."

I thanked him for his kindness.

The boys from the Third came up with a truck to get me, but they gave me bad news, which they had been keeping back. My mother had died in Toronto. It was a terrible blow to me, and I thought over what she had said when I left Toronto: "I will never see you again."

The boys had collected the food parcels that had come for me from Regina, Toronto, and England, so when they got me to our park at Olhain, they decided to have a party. It was some party! I was lucky to get a small piece of cake.

We picked up supplies at Aubigny, Bray, Barlin, etc., and took them up to a point near the front. Commanders did not want many trucks on the road, so often we would work nights. It was very difficult driving in the dark. The trees had all been destroyed on each side of the road, so it was a case of watching the stumps to stay on the road.

Our trucks did all kind of jobs. We were attached to the tunnellers, who were a hardy lot. We would take the tunnellers up as close to the line as we could, then they would carry their equipment into the trench. We would then take a shift back and bring in another. It kept us busy.

These different actions went on until Christmas, when

there was a sort of an armistice—no firing, but each side watched the other.

Tunnelling company at the Somme, 1916 (via BBC.com).

Our officers decided to have a party in a big barn at Tilloy. We bought a few kegs of French beer, and there were all kinds of Scotch, rye, gin, brandy, etc.

I remember our cook, Jack Henderson, stirring the hot brandy sauce for the plum pudding. He was clearly high.

I said, "Jack, that's pretty strong brandy."

He said, "It's the fumes, Sam."

The *Daily Mail*, a London newspaper, had sent Christmas puddings, the best you could buy, over to France for all the Canadian troops.

The men got pretty high and started getting after our officers, especially the OC (I won't give you his name) with abusive remarks. He left and got soldiers from an English regiment in the next town to chase us out of the hall.

Did this regiment have a good time! They ate everything in sight and drank any liquor that was left. In the morning our troops went over to have a drink of beer, and every keg was empty, so they had to suffer with a big head.

9

VIMY RIDGE

After the so called "holiday season," the Canadian divisions started getting ready for the Vimy Rush. We were driving to all the different railheads, collecting different supplies as they were required. We had no knowledge of where we would be going from day to day.

Because I was able to speak a little French, I was chosen to go out of our district to get matériel or to do other errands. One job I had was going to Barlin to get the rum for the troops. The driver of the truck took sick, so I had to go alone, with the credentials.

It was getting dark when I reached our park. I had not eaten since breakfast at 6 a.m. I therefore went to our staff sergeant and told him the truck was loaded with rum and he should put guards on it. He told me to be the guard, but I said, "I am going to the cookhouse to see if I can get something to eat."

I was under the impression that he had enough sense to guard the truck!

Some of the fellows took me to an *estaminet* for a French beer, which is very low in alcohol, but when I was not looking they poured rum in my glass. Since I didn't drink liquor I didn't know the difference, and consequently I went into semi-darkness. They then took me to an empty truck, put me in the back, and placed blankets on top of me.

The next morning, I didn't know what had happened. I had breakfast and then drove the truck to deliver the goods at a crossroad, where the four brigades came to pick up their quota.

We had one of our officers and the staff sergeant, whom I had told to guard the truck, there to see to the sharing of the rum; but as soon as they opened the tarpaulin and lifted the boxes, which should have contained two gallons of rum, they realized they were empty.

Our officer demanded from the first driver what happened, and of course he said he had been sick, and I was the driver.

I told them I had taken the truck into our park and told the staff sergeant to put guards on it.

The staff sergeant admitted I had told him to put guards on, but he had had the regular guards on night duty.

The whole matter was hushed up, and when I got back to

the park, I sure gave the troops the devil for what they had done.

They said, "What are you kicking about? We have your share."

I said, "I don't want it, keep it."

That was the end of the rum vanishing. I had to keep my mouth shut; you don't tell on one another or about such pranks.

I was on another rum and confidential trip. I had lived a sheltered life, but now I was getting an education on how the other side of life managed.

Canadian soldiers advancing through German wire entanglements at Vimy Ridge, April, 1917 (Department of National Defense, Library and Archives Canada PA-001087).

The Battle of Vimy Ridge started on March 20, 1917. The pounding of the barrage, eighteen-pounders and seven- and nine-inch howitzers, for two weeks was like thunder all the time. Finally, at 5:30 a.m. on April 9, the Canadian attack started.

What a wonderful job our infantry (four divisions) did! They took the towns of Vimy and Petit-Vimy, and the hill looking down into the city of Lens. The road to Arras was open. The Thélus woods were just stumps.

We were moved up to a town near Mont-Saint-Eloi. All that was left of this town was one wall of the church.

The post office for the troops was moved to a place between La Targette and Arras, where a huge German dugout that had been captured became the headquarters for the remainder of the battle.

Jack Brant's truck was ordered to be the mail truck and he chose me to be his second driver. We had to collect the mail from all the divisions and brigades. We took the first lap at night to the coast, stayed overnight at the different points, and then brought in the last lap of the mail to the post office.

Everything was fine for a while, until Jack, who was feeling high, dropped the truck into a cellar at Carency. I had to take over after the MP ordered him to get in the back of the truck with the guard, while the mail corporal sat with me. We were ordered back to our park and an investigation was held.

For punishment, Jack's truck was given the job of bringing all the dirty garments to Saint-Moreil for cleaning. Of course, they were lousy. I finally got relieved after I had my share of vermin.

I did different jobs until I felt I needed a change. I had

written an application to join the Royal Flying Corps when I was in England, but for some reason an old colonel had turned me down. I decided to try again.

I had to have the recommendation of three officers. I got my company lieutenant, my chemistry teacher from Tech, and Captain Stewart, my running mate from Regina, to sign my paper. My application was considered, and I was sent to Le Bélieu for an interview. I was accepted, but had to wait until General Haig's headquarters gave notice to report.

10

UNDER FIRE AT PASSCHENDAELE

The Battle of Vimy Ridge was coming to an end, and all the Canadian divisions were being moved to the Ypres front. The Third Battle of Ypres, also called the Battle of Passchendaele, was on. It started on July 31, 1917, and ended on November 10.

It was terrible; the canals were all damaged and the ground was just a quagmire of mud.

The Army engineers built roads, over the mud, out of wooden railroad sleepers (ties), with a four-by-four rail on each side so our trucks would not slip off into the mud. When we wanted to turn around, we had to pick a firm place to get our front wheel over the four-by-four, but never let our rear wheels off the sleeper. It was back and forth until we got around.

Mud, water, and barbed wire: the terrain at Passchendaele (Canadian War Museum 19930013-511).

One night the Germans cut the road with shell fire and four trucks were given the job of taking up a load of stone to fill the holes.

I was the lead truck, with a corporal in charge. The Germans saw us and started firing artillery shells. They were missing, but the ground was so wet we were showered with mud. My corporal and the labour gang who were to unload the truck got super nervous and beat it into a German pillbox our troops had captured. The other three trucks did not come up: they returned to their base and reported I was in trouble.

Here I was, left with a truck full of stones. I got out of the truck and inspected the hole, and decided I would straddle it. When I got to the other side, you never saw a load of stone come off so quickly.

I got turned around, drove over the stones, and shouted to the corporal that if he wanted a ride to come out—which he did, crying and yapping his head off. I told him to shut up.

He said, "Will you report me for what I did?"

I said, "I will not."

Then I was stopped by a stretcher-bearer sergeant to take the wounded to the first medical hut. My corporal would not stop his noise, which got my wind up. I started going too fast, until the sergeant who was in the truck told me to slow down, as the injured soldiers were dying. I slowed down. I was never under such a strain in all my life.

When we got to the medical hut the wounded soldiers were attended to as well as the medical attendants could do. My truck and I were commandeered by the medical unit. I looked around for my corporal, but he had vanished.

After several trips they allowed me to go. By then it was getting dark. When I got to Saint-Julien, my officer was there and asked me where I had been. I told him.

He said, "Are you all right?"

I said, "Yes."

He left me, and I got back to the park. After I got something to eat, a delegation of my chums told me that the Australians wanted to buy me a beer.

I said, "What for?"

They said, "For what you did today. Some of the wounded you brought down were Aussies."

Australian Infantry wounded around a blockhouse near the site of Zonnebeke Railway Station, October 12, 1917, Battle of Passchendaele. The sunburst was captured separately and added to the image for effect (photo by Frank Hurley, from National Library of Australia - la.pic-an24574133).

I went over to have a drink with them and they made a great fuss over me. One of the privates was an Australian millionaire. He told the barmaid to bring a pitcher of beer. She brought in a little jug. He told her to bring in the wash-stand jug full of beer. We sure had a merry night!

One time during the Battle at Passchendaele, I was loaned with my truck to the Second Divisional Ammunition Column. While at Wijtschate Corner (*Willshay in original; this is my best guess. – Ed.*), we saw our aeroplanes were all beating it away from the line. We could not make out what was happening, but we found out. The German bomber planes, protected by their fighter planes, were over us, dropping bombs on the ammunition dump. (This was during the time the Germans had supremacy of the air.)

Troops unloading howitzer shells from a truck (Canadian War Museum 19920044-617).

I was sitting in my truck while the troops were unloading the shells. I looked around and saw them all running toward a dugout. I started after them right away, and just in time. Just as I got inside a bomb dropped at the entrance, on a pile of cordite, and, of course, it went up in flames. We were pushed against the opposite wall of the dugout to escape the flames and fumes.

These troops in the labour battalions were shellshocked soldiers who had done their stint in the trenches. They started to shout and carry on, and believe me, I was scared. I said, "Fellows, I am not going to stay here. I am going to run through the flames. If you want to live, follow me and take your chances outside."

I started through the flames. Fritz was certainly dropping the bombs. I saw an officer behind a pile of shells, so ran there and got beside him. Whenever a bomb exploded, we ducked.

After a while, all was quiet. The aeroplanes had left. The fellows in the dugout were okay. The damage was to the cordite pile and my truck: a bomb had dropped in front of it and shattered the radiator. I couldn't even find the pieces. It had come disconnected from the engine at the top and bottom hose inlets.

I could not see anything else wrong, so I said to myself, "I wonder if the engine will start." I got my crank and gave it a swing, and sure enough, the engine started.

I immediately stopped the engine, got a piece of wood, shaped it to the size of the bottom inlet, took my handkerchief, wrapped it around the wood plug, and then drove it into the engine outlet. Then I got an empty two-gallon Shell

Company gasoline can, filled it with water out of a shell hole, made a cardboard funnel, and poured the water in the top inlet. Not a drop leaked at the bottom.

The officer signed for my load and said, "Goodfellow, you are lucky."

I said, "So are you."

He said, "You don't know what I mean. Look at the back of your seat."

I took a look: a piece of shrapnel had torn the back to pieces, right where I had been sitting. I realized my guardian angel was looking after me!

I said good-bye and started home with my damaged truck. I could only go about a hundred yards before I had a steaming engine. I would jump out and fill the engine again. When the troops jumped onto my truck I would say, "Fellows, please get off. I don't want any more load. Look what I am nursing home to the base."

I had to fill that engine a number of times before I got to our parking place, which was the other side of Poperinge. I thought, *Now I will get a rest till my truck gets a new radiator*, but no luck.

They had a new truck for me in the morning.

11

INTO THE FLYING CORPS

I got into other hair-raising experiences, and finally I went to our staff sergeant (the one I mentioned in the story about the stolen rum) and asked him why I got all the dangerous jobs to do.

He said, "You are going to the Flying Corps, and we don't want anybody else killed. We don't mind you getting killed because we are going to lose you anyway."

I said, "Isn't that nice!"

I made it my business to find out if my paper had come through to go to the Royal Flying Corps. It had, but this staff sergeant was keeping me as long as he could.

There was another driver who was going to the RFC, a fellow named Blanchford, from Providence, Rhode Island. When we brought the matter to the attention of our officer, we were sent on our way in a cattle car to General Haig's headquarters at Hesdin. An officer interviewed us, and then we left for Bologne.

After reaching Dover, we boarded the train for Farnsborough, which was the recruiting centre for the Royal Flying Corps. We stayed at this place for a few days and then we departed for Hastings, which was where the Flying Corps decided whether you would be a pilot or observer or returned to your original unit as not suitable to be a flyer.

I went to London with my flight but was turned down as a fighter pilot. Instead, I was to be an artillery observer. I was very disappointed. I made an appointment with our OC and asked to be allowed to go to the RFC medical centre for another examination.

I went to London with the next flight, was re-examined, and was turned down *again* as a pilot. I asked the doctor why.

He informed me my nerves were not very good. "You are from France?" he said.

I said, "Yes."

He asked what had happened, and I told him about the German bomb raid at the ammunition dump. He said, "I passed you as an observer because I figured that when you are through your course, you will be in good health. I know you would make a good fighter pilot, but your dizziness might affect you in training."

I decided I would be the best artillery observer in the RFC.

H astings was a summer holiday point for the natives. We were housed in one of the houses there. What a mistake! Instead of us sleeping in beds, the landlady bought cots, and had us cadets sleeping in the attic. The bathroom, toilet, etc., were in the basement.

Hastings in 1916 (from an old postcard).

You should know the British always saw to it that *their* forces received sufficient rations, but we didn't get our correct food. The landlady was filling up her house with summer boarders and using *our* food to feed them!

We never mixed with her boarders and we ate in a different room. She would take our bread, and cut it into dices, the same size as a lump of sugar. We were only allowed a few dices. The rest of the food would not feed a pigeon.

As colonials from France, we knew there was something wrong. The native boys would not complain, so we went to our sergeant-major and flight officer, and told them what was happening. They said they would investigate.

When you were eating in a barrack, the officer of the day would come in and ask if there were any complaints. The officers made an excuse to visit the boarding house at dinner time and asked if we had any complaints. We colonials made the complaint in front of the landlady. The officer opened the door of the visitors' dining room and saw what they were eating, then he visited our sleeping quarters, etc.

He told the landlady in a few words that the matter would be investigated, and then he left. She knew she was in for it and gave us the devil.

The next day we were moved to a barrack. The landlady was informed that she was in trouble with the military for stealing food and would not be allowed to have any more cadets.

Most of our training was drilling and physical exercise—trying to weed out the unfits—and on how an officer should conduct himself. There was one lecture I will always remember on personal hygiene, and what to see and what not to see. This served me in good stead when I became a commissioned officer.

After a short term, we observers-to-be were moved to St. Leonard's, where our course really started.

12

AN ADVANCED COURSE

It was a hard course. The instructor sure put us through our paces: up at 5 a.m., and drilling on the beach from 5:30 to 6 a.m., with the wind blowing in from the sea. They were getting rid of the cadets who could not take it. We took a little of everything that we would need when we became observers.

We had an examination and the ones who got over a certain mark (200 of us) were moved to Bath. After we had been in Bath for a short time, we were given another examination. We saw that it was the same examination we had written at St. Leonard's. We told the examiner, who was from headquarters in London. He immediately phoned London.

He came back and told us, "Your group has been lost. You will stay here in Bath to take a more advanced course."

The Royal Air Force had been formed on April 1, 1918. Since this combined the Royal Flying Corps with the Royal Naval Air Service, we got some subjects dealing with naval warfare.

However, we were still under the Royal Flying Corps military section for discipline, and our head commanding officer was Colonel Rooke. His nickname was the Mad Clown of Bath. We would ride around in his car, sitting in the back seat, and if he saw a cadet who was not carrying his cane parallel to the ground, he would get up on the back seat and shake his fist at the poor cadet.

Our instructors were injured flyers. They knew nothing about the theory of flying or the subjects they were supposed to teach.

I will mention only one example of the lack of knowledge some of these instructors had. We called this instructor Split Ass Charlie, for all he talked about when he was supposed to be teaching us a subject was his acrobatics in the air when he was a fighter pilot. He had been shot down and suffered a concussion.

He was to give us instructions on aerial photography. He started talking about the camera, and the cadet next to me said, "Do you know what he is talking about?"

The instructor immediately said, "What are you talking about?"

The cadet said, "I don't understand your remarks about the camera."

The instructor told him, "Neither do I. Does the cadet

you were talking to understand the theory of the camera?" Then he asked me directly. "Do you?"

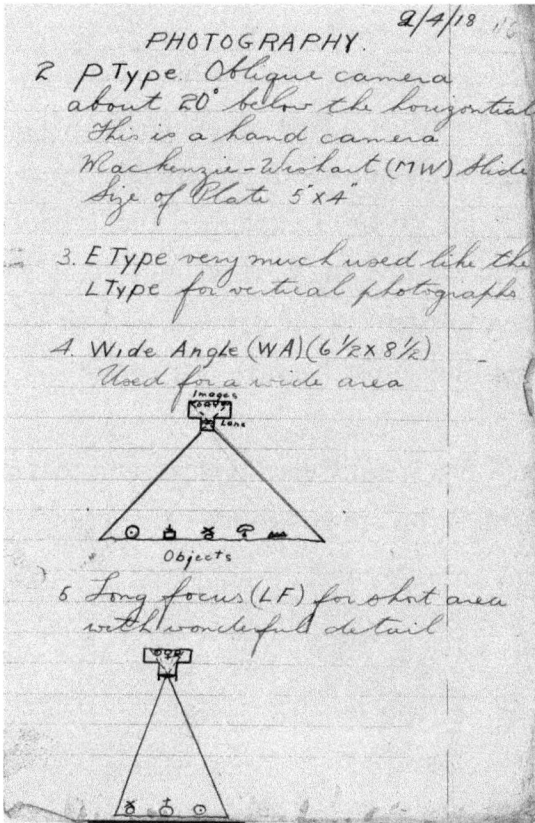

A page from Sam's notebook dealing with photography.

I said, "Yes."

"All right, you come up here and take over." He went and sat in a seat.

I started out by telling the class that light travels in a straight line and any correction is done by the lens, convex or concave, which I illustrated by making a drawing on the board. Then I said that when you take a picture, the film impression or picture is upside down to the object.

Right away the instructor shouted at me to stop pulling their legs.

I said, "O.K., I will prove it," which I did by making a sketch on the board of a tree and then drawing lines to a camera through the lens and focal point, etc.

He then let me go on. I explained that when they were taking an aerial picture, the farthest point they were taking was the closest to them in the camera, and vice versa, so to get everything they must be sure to overlap the images on the films.

He thanked me, dismissed the class, and told me to stay behind. He said, "Who are you to have that knowledge?"

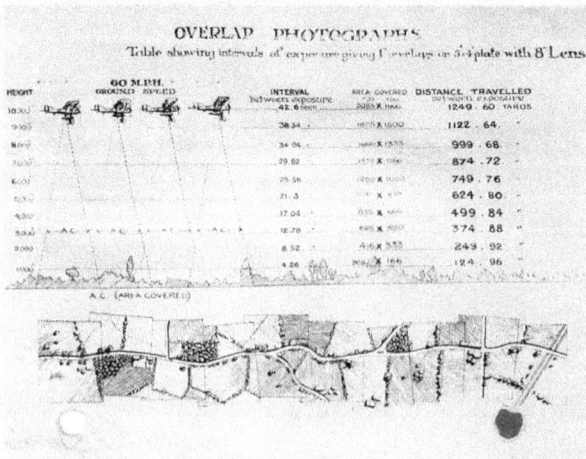

A handout detailing the taking of overlapping aerial photographs for reconnaissance.

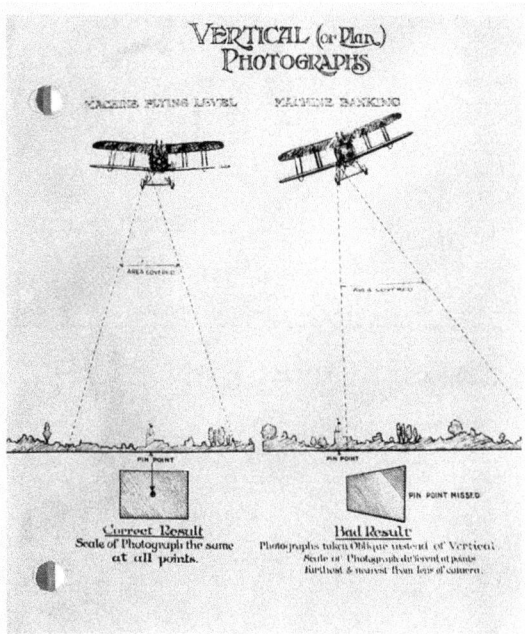

*Another handout explaining why it is important for the
aircraft to be flying straight and level while taking aerial
photographs.*

I said, "I am a Technical High School student, studying to
be an engineer."

They didn't get that training in their schools, and there
were other subjects that they did not get. The information
soon got around among the instructors, so that if they didn't
know a subject, they would ask me. I became conversant or
knowledgeable on a subject by buying a book on the subject
and studying it. Therefore, I kept well-informed on the
subject of flying.

13

BAD TROUBLE IN BATH

While at Bath, I got into trouble through no fault of my own.

We had to line up at a large pavilion for dinner at 7:30 p.m. We lined up as on parade and marched into the dining room.

A one-legged pilot was officer of the day. He was standing at the front. A few cadets behind me were talking and he pointed at me and told me to stop talking.

I said, "Sir, I am not talking."

He told the cadet corporal to take my name. I was to appear at my flight orderly room for talking on parade.

The corporal didn't report me. He came up to me a few days later and told me the pilot officer wanted me punished.

I said, "O.K., report me," which he did, and next day I was

brought up at 10 a.m. in front of my flight officer, Captain Montmorency, a South African infantry officer.

He read the charge and right away he said, "Two days, CB (confined to barracks)."

I said, "Sir, I am not guilty; I didn't do anything."

Immediately he said, "Appear at squadron orderly room at 11 p.m."

They put guards over me, and marched me to Colonel Rooke's orderly room, where I was put on trial for disobedience.

The orderly officer read the charge and Colonel Rooke called me a "damn Canadian bastard" and a "foreign son of a bitch," and every filthy name in his vocabulary.

I could stand no more and I started to call him the same names. He told one of his sergeants to grab me, but he could not handle me.

Then he had four of his NCOs grab me, one on each leg and one on each arm, and throw me to the ground. He then pronounced the sentence: twenty-one days confined to barracks, put in jail and drilled at the double, and returned to the Canadians after I had done my sentence, as I was not fit to be an officer in the Royal Air Force.

I got up off the floor and he shook his fist at me and called me names, and they handed me over to my flight sergeant major.

We left the orderly room under guarded escort. When we got outside the sergeant major said, "Why did you get into this trouble?"

I said, "I didn't do anything, but the cadets who were carrying on were not men enough to take the blame and I don't take punishment for anything I have not done."

When we got down to our quarters, the sergeant major said, "I have no jail to put you in. I know what I will do with you—I have an empty attic in one of the houses." We went there and he said, "I will lock you in here."

I said, "If you do, I will meet you on the steps downstairs."

The guards laughed, and the sergeant major asked me to repeat what I had said.

I took him to the window. "See that rain pipe? I will climb down."

He said, "You little devil, I believe you would! What am I going to do with you?"

I said, "I will give you my word of honour, I will stay here if you do not lock the door."

"Very well," he said, "I will trust you."

He and the guards left.

I sat on the floor feeling sorry for myself. After a lapse of time, the sergeant major came back and said, "You are to stay in your own quarters and attend classes."

We went down, and I returned to my quarters.

I got fed up and wrote a letter asking to be returned to France to my unit, the Third. I gave it to Captain Montmorency. He took it to Colonel Rooke; they decided to give me back my letter and that I had to complete my sentence.

After classes, I would report at the Bath Cricket Grounds and five officers would take turns at drilling me at the double. They would wear themselves out and another would take over. They would shout at me, "We will take that sneer off your face!"

I would say to myself, *Like the devil you will!*

They would put cadets behind me who had misbehaved and got two days or more CB. After a few minutes, they would faint and fall to the ground, but they would keep me going, hoping I would fall. I was in wonderful shape.

After I had done my twenty-one days, they paraded me to the flight orderly room and Captain Montmorency asked me for my letter to return to my unit. I told him I had torn it up. He told me to write it out. I said I would not because the Canadian Ten had prevailed on me to stay.

Captain Montmorency said, "We will send you back. Colonel Rooke does not want you here and you know what happened to you."

"Yes, but I was innocent."

Colonel Rooke went to the captain who was the chief technical instructor from London, hoping for a bad report on my knowledge.

The captain asked him to repeat the name. Told it was "Goodfellow," the captain said that headquarters in London would think he was crazy, because I was the only cadet who had a mark of 100. (I got this information from the Women's Royal Air Force girls in the office.)

The "old devil" (as the guards called him) tried his best to remove me from the RAF, but failed.

There was a draft going to Reading and I was put on the

draft, not as a cadet officer but as a cadet sergeant, along with another cadet named Clayton—a boy from a prominent English family and from one of the universities.

The other cadets would not talk to us as we were to be non-commissioned. I gave them the devil and told them what I thought of the English.

We arrived at Reading and marched in, and names were checked. The sergeant major called off the officer cadets and then called off Clayton's name and my name. He said, "Cadets for sergeant, two steps in the rear," and then dismissed us.

Cadet Clayton started to cry. I told him to stop it and come with me.

I went up to the regimental sergeant major and told him the story of what had happened at Bath. I gave him Colonel Rooke's name.

"That old devil, I was in his regiment, the Middlesex, and I have it in for him," he said. He took out his pen and scratched out our names at the bottom of his list of cadets and inserted them in the correct place with the officer cadets.

He then shouted for the cadets to fall in, which they did. He read off the names and of course, they all shouted present. Clayton and I shouted present in loud voices.

The sergeant major dismissed the cadet flight. I said to Clayton, "Do you want a holiday to go and tell your people?"

He said, "Yes. Will you come with me?"

I went up to the RSM and said, "Sir, could Clayton and I have a few days' holiday?"

He looked at his list, checked our marks, and said, "You damn Canadians don't know when you are well off. Come with me."

He went to the orderly room to talk to the OC and came out with two railway warrants. He said, "Do you have any money?"

We said, "Yes."

"Then you don't want to see the paymaster."

We said, "No."

It was Friday at noon. He said, "If you two little devils are not back by twelve o'clock midnight Sunday, I will skin you both alive. Now, beat it, and good luck, boys."

He was the finest NCO that I met all the time I was in the force.

We were back on time.

14

A NON-MILITARY ENGAGEMENT

During one of my trips to Hanley to see Nancy, we became engaged. It happened this way:

Stoke-on-Trent is in the Potteries and is a very smoky place. They call it the Five Boroughs. As well as making pottery and fine china, they had a number of coal mines.

In the early days it was a question: should the factories be at the coal mines, or in Wales, where the finest clay came from? It was decided to have the factories at the mines on account of the movement of the material required in the firing of china and pottery. The clay was brought to the Potteries by barge via the canals and railroad.

The same decision faced Andrew Carnegie when it was decided to have the steel mills in Pennsylvania (Pittsburgh and Scranton) and bring the iron ore there from wherever they could find it.

I have been through a steel mill: the Lackawanna Steel Plant at Lackawanna, New York, on Lake Erie near Buffalo. I was invited to go by the graduating engineering students from the School of Practical Science at the University of Toronto. During my apprenticeship I had some of them as my helpers, because they had at that time to do some practical work before graduation.

It was a wonderful sight, seeing the ore and coal being unloaded from the boats, mixed with the scrap, and then put in the large swing-hinged cupola and coming out in liquid form. It was allowed to cool, chemically tested, and then preheated and rolled into train rails and other shapes.

Nancy took me to several places in Staffordshire. One was Lake Rudyard. You could not find a more beautiful place.

I rented a boat, since I was a good oarsman, having rowed on Lake Ontario and Wascana Lake in Regina. Away we went, Nancy in the bow and me near the stern, and I thought, *Now is the time for me to pop the question.*

I asked Nancy if she would marry me, and after a smile she said, "Yes."

I then asked her if I would have to ask her dad.

She said, "Well, it is customary."

So, it was agreed that I would speak to her dad as soon as we got back.

We beached the boat, and then I kissed my future wife for the first time. Then we got in the boat and got back to Hanley as fast as we could. I was the happiest man in England.

Lake Rudyard, Staffordshire, as it appears today (Wikimedia Commons).

I might say here I would have preferred a running-away marriage at Gretna Green and to have had the old blacksmith marry us. I detested the thought of asking Nancy's Dad, for I knew, him being a great joker, that I would get the works, which I did.

Nancy, the devil, got in the house before me, and gave the show away, because she wanted to be in the fun.

Did I get it! He wouldn't give his consent. We were all cannibals and savages in Canada and he didn't want his daughter in such a country. He kept his face as solemn as he could. Nancy and her mother were behind the door, in the other room, laughing fit to kill, and at last their laughter was so great we heard them, and then Dad and I started laughing. He gave his consent.

I finally came down to earth and hugged my future wife. The date was set for after the war. (It took place January 2, 1919.)

Anne Owen "Nancy" Ridgway.

15

TOP OF THE CLASS

We were moved to Reading, where our course was plotting the ground for the artillery.

They had a field laid out in sections of the whole alphabet, wired with lights. We cadets would go up to a tower, sit in aeroplane fuselages, and, when we saw the lights, Morse-code the letters to the ground examiner. Clayton and I had a perfect score, the highest in the flight, and the OC and the RSM were very pleased with us.

When we were through with our training at Reading, we left for the Isle of Sheppey, which is an island in the Thames estuary, for training in machine gunning and types of fuses attached to bombs.

When our cadet squadron left the Isle of Sheppey, we went to Hythe in Kent to finish off our training.

The Air Force first moved us into the Hythe Hotel, and

our training consisted of complete map reading, including topography; also, faults to be encountered with the Lewis machine gun. We were then moved to the Hythe Aerodrome for flying, to find out if we could take it.

There was a grating where the observer stood or sat, so that if you were sick the mess would drop into the air. The saying was, "Who put the marmalade on the fuselage?"

When my turn came, I climbed in and got on my seat. The pilot looked at me. I said, "Go to it." He started, and I looked down through the grating. The Earth seemed to be running into us instead of us going over the ground.

The training pilots took no sympathy on you. Once you were in the air you got the works: they were doing their best to make you sick or call stop. They did loop-the-loops, which made you think the earth was coming up to meet you, as well as somersaults, upside-down flying, side-slipping, and the Immelmann, which made you wonder which way you were going.

My flying coat seemed to be around my ears, but I had it belted to my legs and I didn't fall out. (It became a famous coat.)

The pilot looked around at me to see if I had turned green, and I said, "How about going through it again? Those maneuvers were wonderful!"

"You have been in France, so you know how to keep your mouth shut," he said. "I am going to land in a field and have a smoke."

He had a smoke, and we had a good chat. He gave me a

lot of tips about what to do if I was picked as a fighter in a two-seater aeroplane.

I spun the propeller and got in, then we were in the air, and soon landed. When I got out he shook my hand and he said, "You're okay." He gave me 100 percent.

We then went to New Romney, which was along the Kent coast, for our final training, which was flying and shooting with camera guns. I passed again okay, shot all my opponents, and got okay again.

The final day came: whether we were to be a commissioned officer or a noncommissioned officer (NCO—a sergeant or a corporal).

We lined up on the flying field, approximately 200 cadets in all. The commanding officer gave us a talk. He told us our marks from all our courses had been tabulated, and our rank would be read out.

He started, and the first name called out was Cadet Goodfellow, number one in the class. I wondered what was going to happen to me. Was I going to be kept in England as an instructor?

He then called out nine more names, and said, "You ten cadets will not be commissioned, but will become flying cadets, and will now be trained as night navigators. You will remove the white ribbon from your hat and wear a full Sam Brown belt. You will leave immediately for Stonehenge to begin training."

He then read out the names of the second lieutenants,

sergeants, and corporals, and then gave us our observer's flying single wing.

The flying cadets and second lieutenants were given the sum of fifty pounds. Before I left New Romney, I purchased the new RAF uniform. (This uniform is now in the Royal Canadian Air Force museum in Ottawa.) It was khaki in colour. Soon after they changed the colour to French blue.

16

COURT-MARTIAL

The ten of us left for Stonehenge to begin our navigation course. It was a terrible course. The theoretical part was very difficult and you had to be on your toes all the time because the flying instructors gave you no mercy.

The actual flying was wonderful. We were supplied with drift indicators to lay out our course and taught how to use them. I got so proficient that I learnt to use them as a slide rule.

They would tell us where to go, such as Southampton, Oxford, or Winchester. It was up to us to ask the pilot what altitude he wanted to fly at. After that we were finished with him: we got no help from him. We went to the atmospheric hut and got the direction of the wind at the correct altitude and miles per hour. We then calculated our course on the drift calculator and gave it to the pilot: the degrees to and from the target.

Before leaving the aerodrome, we would check the wind direction and speed of the wind, as sometimes it changed very quickly and then we had to make a quick calculation and inform the pilot of the new information.

Then, away we would go. I was always lucky enough to get over the target and reach home base exactly.

Stonehenge Aerodrome from the air (english-heritage.co.uk).

One time we flew late at night to Oxford and went over the University, which was our target.

We reached home base and were halfway to landing when I saw a new Handley Page bomber was doing the same. I just caught it in time and waved my arm to the left. The pilot got our vee-type pusher plane out of the way.

We passed the aerodrome, just about touching some of

the hangars, with the pilot trying to land. I could see the top of the trees. He went on, and suddenly we hit the ground, a few feet from an infantry trench. Had we hit the trench I would have been thrown, but the pilot would have been killed, with the engine on top of him.

A Royal Aircraft Factory FE2b with a "vee" undercarriage. This is probably the type of aircraft Sam almost crashed in; he would have been riding in the cockpit at the very front (Wikimedia Commons).

I got out my Very pistol, which was loaded with the colours of the day, and fired. After an hour they located us and drove us to our base.

The pilot was complimented for his quick action in evading an accident. He said, "Don't thank me, thank Cadet Goodfellow."

The Handley Page was one of the new Handley Pages with two 360-horsepower engines instead of the standard

250-horsepower engines. There would have been the devil to pay if it had been wrecked!

The next adventure I had came about because of a cadet who had got his wind up at night flying and asked me would I take his place. I said okay and climbed into the vee-type pusher plane.

Along came an instructor, who said, "What are you doing up there?"

I said, "I was taking Cadet So-and-So's place. Someone in his family is sick."

"Like hell you are! Get out of the plane. The pilot here is going up to do his solo night landing." Did I jump out of the plane presto! Quick!

The poor pilot was dead a few minutes after take-off. He hit a fence and the engine crushed him.

Fools like me never learn.

The next episode was terrible, and nearly ended my career as a flyer.

I had been out night flying. When we landed, I checked in on the aerodrome log book where I had been and the time returned—10:50 p.m.—and got ready for my cot.

Next morning there was a corporal guard at my cot, who informed me I was required at the OC orderly room. I dressed in my Royal Flying Corps uniform, then they marched me to the orderly room. I began to think, *What is this all about?*

I soon found out. The OC acquainted me with the fact that I was under arrest for shooting up a village, chasing a buggy with a man and his wife inside, shooting up a house as visitors were leaving, and worst of all, shooting King George V's horse breeding stable, taking slates off the roof.

Whoo, what a charge!

"Sir, I did nothing of the kind," I said. "I was flying and shooting at the white target and split it right down the middle and never touched the Lewis gun again."

He would not have it, and informed me that King George wanted me court-martialed on a certain date, and that the King was to be informed of the trial.

They took away my Sam Brown belt, and then I became a prisoner—what they called "undressed." (If I had been an officer, they would have taken my insignia from my cuffs and shoulders.) They then marched me out and put guards over me all the time, but allowed me to attend classes.

They had different officers interrogating me with different questions, trying to cross my statements, wanting me to admit I was guilty. They had one old colonel questioning me in front of a map showing me the way I had supposedly flown, with the degrees and data sheet.

I told him that was wrong and pushed his hand away

from the map. Then I showed him how I *really* flew that night.

He said, "You are a very headstrong young man, the type we want in the air force, but it is bad you are in this trouble. The King wants you punished, and we can't do anything about it."

The British military are a peculiar people, for when you are in trouble, they ostracize you. I was in an awkward position, because I was the only Canadian at the aerodrome.

There was an Australian, but he would not talk to me. I wanted him to compare the rifling of my Lewis gun with a bullet from the shooting. He just ignored me.

I can tell you I was in a terrible mental condition, knowing it was not me, but unable to get any evidence to help me.

The day of the court martial arrived. I arrived at the ante-room and marched in under guard. All the witnesses were there. They looked at me as if I were a criminal. They certainly took care they had enough witnesses on *their* side, but here was me alone among a bunch of foreigners. What they would say against me was beyond my imagination.

Then, all at once, the heavens opened and an angel came to my rescue!

A young sergeant came up to me while I waited with guards around me to march me in to hear my fate. The sergeant said to me, "Sir, I am very sorry to have to appear against you."

I said, "Sergeant, tell the truth, for they are forcing this on me." I left him and walked to the other end of the anteroom, and then said to myself, *What can the sergeant say about me?*

I went back to him and said, "Sergeant, what are you going to say against me?"

He said, "Sir, I am the timekeeper of this aerodrome and I wrote down the time you shot up our town."

I said, "I didn't shoot up your town. What time was it?"

He said, "I wrote it down at the time, and here it is, 11:10 p.m."

I said, "Are you certain?"

"Certainly, I am sure."

I said, "Stay where you are and don't let anyone have that paper."

I then went to the sergeant with his guard at the court-martial door, and told him I wanted to speak to my lawyer officer (whom I had never seen).

The sergeant said, "No! The trial is about to begin."

I said, "Sergeant, I am going in if I have to fight the bunch of you."

He got scared and sent in one of his airmen to inform the court-martial chairman what I wanted.

Out came my lawyer officer, a pompous devil, and said, "What do you want?"

I said, "I want you to come over and meet this sergeant."

He said, "I won't."

I said, "Yes, you will, if I have to drag you over!"

He really got scared and came over. I said, "Sergeant, show him that paper, but hang on to it." Then I said said to the officer, "What time is on the paper?"

He said, "11:30 p.m. What difference does it make?"

I said, "Go inside and look at the log book and you will see that I checked in at 10:50, ten minutes to 11 p.m. This sergeant is the timekeeper for the aerodrome, and you will see that the pilot checked in the plane at 10:50 p.m. There is a twenty-minute difference."

He said, "The King will be as mad as hell."

"I am not interested about the King being mad!"

He left and went into the court-martial court. Then they asked the sergeant to come in.

They then took the guards off me and asked me to come in. They informed me a terrible mistake had been made, and gave me the Air Force's apology, then gave me my Sam Brown belt.

They checked the records and found the culprit had left the day before the trial, because he would not make navigator and was going as an observer.

I had been under a terrible strain; nearly out of my mind.

The next morning, an airman was at my cot informing me I was to report at the orderly room at once. I said to myself, *What have they got on me now?*

I hurriedly dressed and went with the corporal to the orderly room. As I stood before the OC of the aerodrome, he apologized to me for what I had been through. Then he said, "You cannot stay here. You have made a fool of all my officers."

I said, "Sir, I didn't make a fool of them, they made fools of themselves."

He said, "Don't you speak that way about my officers."

I kept quiet.

He repeated, "You cannot stay here. There will be a plane here at 2 p.m. to take you to Lympne Castle on your way to France. You have a splendid record and the High Command asked me to inform you that you will be gazetted today as a second lieutenant."

"Sir," I said, "I am ready to go now. I have all my things packed."

He said, "Did you know you would have to leave?"

I said, "Yes."

"Well, I will have a plane ready in an hour."

He then got out of his official chair and said, "Goodfellow, I am sorry this happened." He shook hands with me and wished me luck in France.

17

"THE SLAUGHTER WAS TERRIBLE"

At Lympne Castle I was chosen to navigate a plane to the south of France with an Air Force transport pilot. Then I was flown to the pilot pool, near where the Independent Air Force had five night squadrons of Handley Pages, which carried three or four men, one ton of bombs, and four Lewis guns, two forward and two at the rear behind the bomb rack, one shooting up and one shooting down.

When I went in to the pool, I was number 500, but the casualties were so great in the Independent that my turn came in a few days. I was taken to 215 Squadron at Xaffévillers as a night navigator (100 Squadron was on the same aerodrome).

Now I must tell you about the Independent Air Force. It was made up out of the toughest individuals in the RAF. Viscount Hugh Trenchard was the commanding officer in

London. He could call you down for an hour and never repeat himself. His language was terrible.

In the Independent Air Force there were five night squadrons, each with four Handley Page aeroplanes with two 250-horsepower engines, capable of carrying approximately 2,000 pounds. The bomb rack held sixteen 112-pound bombs vertically, or a 500-pound or a 1,000-pound bomb strapped under the middle of the plane.

A Handley Page bomber. These aeroplanes were sixty-two feet long and twenty-two feet tall, and had a wingspan of 100 feet (Library of Congress).

There was also one night squadron that had a mixture of planes that included vees or pusher-types (*again, probably the Vickers FE2b – Ed.*), which had the propeller and engine behind the pilot, with the observer in front. They did not go as far across the line as the Handley Pages and DH.9s. There were also four day-bombing squadrons with DH.9s, who were being equipped with DH.10s.

The slaughter was terrible. One day while I was there a whole squadron of DH.9s were shot down, and very few pilots and observers were alive after the fight. I only met one pilot who survived—he came down on the wing.

When you were with the Independent Air Force, you typically only lasted five or six trips. That was all I made. I will list them from memory, as I have no logbook: Saarbrücken, Thionville (Diedenhofen, as called by the Germans), Karlsruhe (a long trip), Strasbourg, and Écrouves junction on the way back. You didn't last long with the load you carried, 2,000 pounds. Your speed was limited, about eighty miles per hour loaded and 100 miles per hour empty.

One afternoon at dispatching we were informed that our object was Cologne. I looked at my pilot and said, "That's it." This meant the end of our stay with the Independent, because you only had sufficient fuel to get to Cologne, then fly into Holland to be interned.

The pilot and I went to our respective huts and packed up all of our clothes that we did not require for the flight. We addressed them to our people in England via Cox's Bank, which forwarded them on to their destination.

We then took our haversacks over to the canteen and

bought chocolate bars, etc. Our haversacks were then filled with our toilet articles, and then we bid good-bye to our pals and waited for take-off time.

After dinner, late in the evening, approximately 10 p.m., we climbed into our plane. The pilot started his engine and I checked with our observer in the tail. I checked the guns and also checked what bombs we were carrying.

We waited for our call letter to depart (all the other Handley Pages had left). We were still sitting there in the machine when an office orderly came along and said we were not going. Orders had come from headquarters that we were not to attack Cologne.

We did not know, nor did we ever find out, the reason for us not going.

18

"GOOD-BYE, THEY HAVE GOT YOU THIS TIME!"

As I mentioned, our top commanding officer was Viscount Hugh Trenchard, Marshal of the Royal Air Force, and he was a tough individual. He was stationed at HQ in London, and came over to France to find out what was happening: why the night squadrons were not making more trips and the day squadrons were having such trouble.

He found out, but it did not make much difference to him. We were behind the Vosges Mountains and the mist came down so heavily that you could not see where you were going.

He visited all nine squadrons and gave us hell when he visited ours. He had the Duke of York with him, later King George VI, who just stood in the corner. This all happened at flying time, about 11 p.m.

He swore at us, called us liars, and said we dropped our

bombs in the fields near our objective and came back with stories that were not true. He said, "Every plane is going over tonight from five Handley Page squadrons, approximately 100. Don't any of you come back before going to your objective."

He added, "The Handley Page only costs 50,000 pounds, so don't worry: we have lots of planes and lots of flyers to take your place." (Liar!)

I was standing right in front of him when he called us liars and I thought he meant me.

We were told to bomb Écrouves junction, because our High Command knew the Germans were beaten but were afraid they were trying to get as much matériel back as possible and might be trying to settle a new defensive line. Écrouves had a "Y" railroad running into the city: if it was destroyed, it would take time to repair.

Sir Hugh Trenchard

We left our mess to get the latest atmosphere conditions, made a few calculations, ran to our plane, made a quick check of our Lewis guns, got the signal from the tower, and then away. We got up as far as our second lighthouse, then the mist came down. We had to backtrack twice before we located our third lighthouse. Then we set our course for Écrouves.

After we crossed the line, the mist got good and thick. The pilot wanted to turn back, but I said, "No chance."

He said, "I don't know where we are."

I said, "Neither do I, for I can't see any landmarks, but keep going on those degrees and then I will get a bearing."

Then I spied the Moselle River and a steel mill that I had seen before. They were busy closing the tops of the cupolas.

The pilot was not satisfied and still wanted to turn back. I said, "No. No English devil is going to call me a liar or say I am a coward, so keep going."

We traveled a few miles on our degree reading, and then I spied a railroad going the way I expected. I said to the pilot, "When we get near the town, come down low and be ready to keep the nose of the plane down, for I am going to drop the whole bunch of bombs at once. Then circle, and we will go through the town with our machine guns."

We finally reached our point. I had the bomb indicator set and the triggers in each hand. When I had the three wires in sight, I let go.

The pilot had the machine in control, after dropping one 500-pound and eight 112-pound bombs, and the observer was dropping twenty-pound Cooper bombs, a total of twenty-four. The pilot circled the church spire, and then we had three machine guns blazing away.

After a while the enemy started firing at us. We tried our best to get above their range. We could see the trace of bullets passing all around us and wondered when they would hit us.

Then the anti-aircraft guns started at us. We had got as far as the German headquarters for this district and they didn't like that. We sure got our share of shells! They knocked out our two engines and knocked off the lower starboard wing and our undercarriage.

Church tower at Écrouves, as it appears today (Wikimedia Commons).

The pilot shouted at me for the searchlight, but we had no power. I dropped our candle parachute to see the ground. It worked okay, but it drifted away. Down we came.

I said to myself, "Good-bye, they have got you this time!"

It is a peculiar thing: you are not afraid to die—you have been so well-trained it does not bother you.

There was crashing, then *bang!*, the pilot and I were sitting on the ground, with my arm over his shoulder and the searchlight in my hand. Everything was smashed. The tail of the plane was standing nearly vertical. We had landed in a forest and the trees had broken our fall.

I got up, and good! I could walk. The pilot had a broken ankle.

Someone else's Handley Page, shot down by anti-aircraft fire near Saargemünd on August 22, 1918 (source unknown).

I went back to find the observer, but he was not there. I thought, "Poor devil, he must have fallen out." But when I returned he was talking to the pilot, holding him up.

Then the pilot and I had an argument about our location. He said, "Look, I could see our aerodrome!"

"Yes, you can see the lights crossed over the top near our location, but we are in Germany," I said. "I am going to set fire to the machine."

He said, "You better not. A machine was set fire the other night and they were in France. They got into trouble."

Then I heard a whistle and saw smoke from a light railroad, twenty-two-inch gauge. I spotted the track and crawled on my stomach to a point near the track, and when the engine passed me, I saw a German soldier as the driver. I waited, and saw another German as the rear brakie.

I got back to the wreck and was hunting for my phosphorus machine-destroyer on my knees when German soldiers, all around me, suddenly rushed at me with bayonets. I stood up and had bayonets stuck at my waist. They were yelling "Comrade, Comrade," and I put up my hands and said, "Comrade!" Then they pulled their bayonets away.

I looked around for the other two, but they were not there. They took me out of the forest to where they had the pilot and observer. Then they took us to a medical hut and got a nurse and a medical attendant. We had landed in a German cage, where they brought Allied prisoners.

The observer had a great gash across his head, just above his eyes, and the pilot a damaged ankle. They gave them first aid.

In the morning they took the pilot and me to the German headquarters at Dieuze. I never saw the sergeant observer again: the Germans were very military-class regulated.

19

"I WANT YOUR SQUADRON!"

They gave the pilot a chair to sit on, then went after me. They wanted to know my name, my squadron, where I was bombing, etc. I told them my name, and for squadron I gave the RAF.

I was examined by a German intelligence officer, Hauptmann (Captain) Mier. He looked like the Kaiser. "I don't want to know your answer, 'RAF!' I want your squadron!"

All he got out of me was "RAF." (Trenchard had told us the night before just to give "RAF.")

Then he asked me, "What was the make of that new machine that landed at your airport?"

I told him I didn't know.

He said, "Do you know, or are you just a damn fool?"

I said, "Yes." (It was a DH.10, a new design.)

In the midst of this questioning, a German general came

into the room, in all his full-dress regalia. They all stopped and saluted the general. I stood still and did not move.

The general and the captain had a few words, then the captain said to me, "Why did you not salute the general?"

I said, "I didn't know he was a general."

The two had more words and then the captain said, "You salute me!"

I said, "I will not. I am a British officer and I won't salute you."

He tried to hit me. I backed away and he chased me all around the room.

I got back to the place where we had started and said, "Damn you," and warded off his blow, and was about to strike him when other officers behind me grabbed me.

The German general said some words, and then they left me alone except to say, "Are you a British regular or a volunteer?"

I said, "I am a Canadian."

They gave the pilot and me each a slice of white bread and a cup of barley coffee. We were then taken to Saint-Avold, the pilot to the hospital and me to prison. The truck had wooden wheels (no tires), and going over the cobblestones it was bang, bang, bang.

They put me in a room with windows painted on the outside and barred, with a military guard outside, and a Russian batman. Every day for three days they quizzed me, but they got no information from me.

One day a German flying observer had a go at me. I got

more information from him than he got from me. He was from Toronto and had worked in the King Edward Hotel. He was a good sport and gave me 100 cigarettes and five cigars.

I had been told at our squadron to slash my flying boots and leather jacket, etc. They took my coat before I could damage it, but I slashed my boots. (That jacket is the one that is now in the museum in Ottawa.) The Germans did not take them, but they took my Sam Brown belt.

The Russian batman gave me a pair of Russian boots that laced up on the outside. I could not eat the fourth-class food, but he enjoyed it, so they did not know that I had not eaten. He, being a common soldier to the Germans, was half-starved.

I was then ordered to go into the interior of Germany. They took me to the Saint-Avold railroad station. While waiting under guard for the train to arrive, I saw a number of British Tommies at a short distance.

One of them put his fingers to his mouth, giving the sign of a smoker. I nodded my head "yes." One came up and I gave him a cigarette; and then one after the other they came, until I had given away all 100 of the cigarettes the German observer had given me. There were five soldiers left, and I remembered I had five cigars left, so I gave each of them a cigar.

There was a disturbance when they went back to the

others, laughing and shouting. It was a great joke that the last should get the greatest smoke.

A German colonel saw the whole thing happen. He then gave the sergeant major the dickens and ordered him to lock me in the baggage room, which he did. I thought, *Now I will try to escape!*, but no luck—there was a guard at every door and window.

The Saint-Avold railroad station (from an old postcard).

We got on a fourth-class coach and traveled to Saar-brücken. A woman on the station broke through the guards along with others, shouting, *"Flieger! Fleiger!* (Flyer! Flyer!)," and tried to start a riot, hocking to spit in my face. The guards pushed her away, and then closed in on me Roman-style to protect me, holding their rifles at the charge. The people quieted down, since they did not want to be killed or clubbed.

We got on another fourth-class coach and got off at a platform siding at night. The platform was crowded with soldiers going back out of the line.

One of our planes was returning home from a bombing raid. It was a beautiful sight. You could have heard a pin drop. The soldiers were quiet, and believe me, I was quiet.

The train was outside the station with a hood over the smoke chimney. When the plane passed, it was removed. We got on the train, left it at Solingen, then crossed the town, where the German sergeant major took me into a wonderful station. It was fixed up as a beer garden, and he bought me a beer. It was just lovely on an empty stomach.

The station was crowded with soldiers, who were very friendly to me and called me *flieger*. While I was there, a German soldier who spoke fluent English came to my table and asked me if it was true that the British were confiscating the property of all German citizens who had left England to fight for the Fatherland.

I said, "Yes, that is true."

He said, "I am ruined. I own a lot of property in Manchester." He asked me for a souvenir, and I gave him my goggles. You could not see out of them for cracks. I guess I must have damaged them when falling through the trees at Dieuze.

We got on another train, and finally reached Karlsruhe. I was put in a hotel room that had four beds, in solitary confinement.

They kept me there for a few days. I tried to scrape the paint from the window, but no luck, the window was painted on the outside. However, there was about an eighth of an inch of space before the paint touched the wood. I nearly got cross-eyed looking through that space!

Then one day they moved me into a room with three infantry officers. Before I could open my mouth, one of them put his fingers to his mouth, giving the signal that the room was wired. We just talked about sports, etc.

After a few days, they took me downstairs before a German major. He said, as I entered the room in front of his desk, "Good day, sir."

I replied, "Good day to you, sir."

He then asked me my name, which I gave him. Then he asked me my squadron.

I said, "RAF."

He said, "I asked for your squadron."

Again, I said, "RAF."

"You won't tell me your squadron?"

I said, "No, sir."

Then I got it. His politeness disappeared. He called me all the names he could get his tongue on, then he said, "You damn Canadians are all alike." He pushed a bell-button and said to the soldier who came in, "Get him the hell out of here."

They marched me along a hall to the outside front door, which was elevated from the street. It was raining.

Outside in the street were pilots and observers waiting for me to appear. As soon as they saw me, it was, "There is Goody, Goody!" and they stampeded. The guards had some trouble keeping them in order.

I went down the steps with my chest out a mile.

20

PRISONER OF WAR

I think the Germans wondered who I was, because they separated me from my cadet friends and I never saw them again. Instead, they put in a hut with infantry officers from different parts of the Commonwealth.

The prison camp in Karlsruhe was in the centre of the city, in a wonderful park that was close to the main street. The prison camp had four barbed-wire fences, with scrambled barbed wire shoulder-high in between. Altogether the fencing would be approximately nine feet wide and eight feet high, with guards all around and a special wire gate.

I made friends with a Captain Hacking, a Rhodesian who had been a South African rugby player and had been given a plantation in Rhodesia at a reasonable price. To keep in physical shape, we had two wooden mallets and a wooden ball, which we knocked to each other.

Karlsruhe Prisoner of War Camp in 1918 (photo by F. Albrecht, State Library Victoria, Australia, Image H40757/5).

The wounded in our hut were in terrible shape. A Scottish captain had got a round of bullets on the lower right side of his waist, and another officer had had his leg and right foot removed. Every Sunday they would cut away the proud flesh and wrap it with toilet paper because they had no bandages. He used to say, "If this war does not get over, I will have no leg left."

The Americans had a wonderful canteen, with an American sergeant in charge. He took a great liking to me and gave me anything I wanted: Nestlé condensed milk, cigarettes, biscuits, candies, chocolate bars, etc. An American soldier, when he came to the camp, got a complete outfit if he wanted it.

The American sergeant in the prison camp at Karlsruhe

had been informed that I was supposed to be taking an American pilot across the line the night after I was shot down. The pilot, an engineering student from Cornell University, had been up in front of our OC for not crossing to his objective, and he had told the OC that his navigator had been an observer who lost himself as soon as he was in the air.

The OC told him he had to go to his objective, and he asked if he could have a trained navigator. The OC asked whom he would like, and he said, "Lieutenant Goodfellow."

The OC said, "You better go and ask him."

He asked me, and I said I would take him over for one night. He then went to the OC and a transfer was given for one operation...but then I was shot down, and it never happened.

The fellows in our hut, when they ran out of cigarettes, would say, "Sam, go and see your American friend and get some smokes."

The meals were terrible, a hunk of fourth-class bread with a cup of burnt-black barley coffee at noon, and a plate of soup that you could pick the leaves out of and another piece of bread at supper—sometimes yes, but most times, no.

We began to get cold, and we were getting colds. The

officers had a meeting and appointed six of us to go see the commander about us getting coats.

A rebellion had broken out, and a soldier committee had taken over all over Germany. The prison commander was still kept in charge, but his rank had been removed from his hat and shoulders.

I was the spokesman. I approached the German sergeant major first and told him I wanted to speak to the commander about giving us coats. He talked to the commander, who agreed to see us. We were marched into his orderly room, saluted him, and told him our request. We put on an act, doing a lot of coughing but not overdoing it.

He told the sergeant major to march us over and give each of us a warm coat. Unknown to us six, the other officers were hiding near the door of the hut, and when the door was opened, they rushed to the entrance. I found myself hitting the opposite wall.

I bent down, grabbed an armful of matériel, stepped sideways, and got out. I discovered I had two leather coats, two canvas sheep-lined one-piece suits, and one bearskin one-piece suit. I gave them all away except one short coat (because I was arranging to escape and I wanted to be able to walk swiftly). I gave them to the wounded, except the long leather coat, which I gave to a New Zealander who was a sheep breeder: he wanted it, because sometimes he slept outside on his plantation.

The day came when we were going to escape. I was number two in the line. Number one got over the last fence, and I was on the top, just going to jump, when a guard raised his gun to shoot the officer who was over. The officer put up his hands and I turned to go in again, shouting at the other officers to beat it.

I went through so fast I tore the coat in several places, but I got into the camp, hurriedly undressed, and got in bed, snoring to pretend I was asleep.

I got away with it.

21

ARMISTICE

While the Armistice was under negotiation, we were allowed to go into town, as long as our senior officer gave his word of honour that we would all return. It was kept, except by one officer, who tried to escape. They caught him, and he was kept in camp.

We had some German money, so we went into a German restaurant called Odgen. The waitress asked us what we would like; of course, we asked, "What do you have?"

She said, "We have some Canadian Club rye."

I nearly fell off my chair. We all had it, along with a piece of German pie, which was awful.

I looked around. There at a table were the officers who had questioned me at Dieuze. They brushed me off when I tried to speak to them.

The next day, we were informed we were going into the

Black Forest. We got on a train and went to Mannheim, which was the opposite direction, but finally we landed in the Black Forest.

The camp was a dirty disgrace. We only spent a few days there, and then departed for Basel, Switzerland. Of course, November 11, 1918, had passed while we were in Karlsruhe.

A Swiss citizen was put in charge of each one of us. I was lucky. The gentleman who was looking after me was the chief engineer for the Switzerland railroad. He took me around, showing me all the different locomotives. He was very proud of his trains.

The Swiss put on a lovely dinner for us and we had a wonderful time. What a change from just across the Rhine! But I must state here it was wonderful coming down the Rhine in the train, seeing all the different castles, ruins, etc.

We left Basel and went through the beautiful valleys, and I noted how the Swiss farmed on the sides of the fertile hills and mountains. The sides were cut out in huge steps, the flat part about twenty-five feet wide, then a rise, then another twenty-five feet, and on up the side of the hill. You could see they were growing all types of vegetation.

We got off at different towns and cities (Dijon looked very Turkish), walked and rode in trucks, and then got on trains again. I don't know how we ate.

We landed at one town, and my pals said, "Sam, you will have lots of money when you get to London."

I said, "I hope so! My lieutenant pay, 10.6, and my pound-a-day flying pay. I hope, anyway."

We were hungry.

We were in front of a French bank. I went in and asked for the manager. He interviewed me, and I told him I would like him to cash a cheque.

He said, "Have you the cheques?"

I said, "No, but I know the number of my account at Cox Bank in London."

He said, "We have no cheques."

I said, "I will make one if you will give me a piece of paper and cash it."

"How much do you want?"

I said, "Ten pounds."

He said, "Very well, I will cash the cheque."

He gave me a piece of brown wrapping paper, and with a rule, I made out a blank cheque, put my Cox Bank number on it, and signed same. He then gave me francs to the value of ten pounds.

The fellows were all delighted. We had enough money to get to Boulogne.

When I got to London, I explained the whole thing to Cox's bank manager, and when I came to Canada, I left ten pounds in my account. Years passed, and Cox Bank asked me to close off my account, because the cheque had not been cashed. The manager thought the French bank manager probably had it framed and was keeping it as a souvenir to show his customers how he had helped out hungry British soldiers.

I said, "Close out the account, but if the cheque ever turns up let me know and I will send you the money." I gave them my address in Regina, but so far, it has not been cashed.

We went through Paris and they gave us a tin of meat. I said to the Australian, "This is certainly lovely chicken."

He said, "Damn fool, it is rabbit!"

I couldn't tell the difference.

22

"A DIRTY-LOOKING DEVIL"

We finally reached Boulogne and got on the boat to Dover. The white cliffs of Dover looked wonderful. When we got off the boat, they were putting twenty-five men to a truck. Hacking was number twenty-five, and they would not let me on because I was number one of the next truck.

I ran after the truck because I had his souvenirs, but I couldn't catch it. I finally sent them to the London office of the Rhodesian Embassy, and I hope he got them. I never heard from him.

We stayed a few days in Dover and then went by train to London. After writing a description of how we were treated by the Germans (all commissioned officers were compelled to do this. I suppose it was a detail all armies required, friend or foe), we were allowed to go to the bank and get some money.

The dining room of the Savoy Hotel, London (English Heritage).

Our group met at a prearranged time and place and went and had dinner at the Savoy Hotel. While we were having our ice cream and strawberries, I heard shouting to my left and my name called. "Sam, Sam, where in hell have you been?"

It was a pilot named Gardner, who was a classmate of mine at Tech and had enlisted from school in the Royal Flying Corps. He was dressed to kill in a Royal Air Force uniform. He had another pilot with him, along with two ladies. They rushed over to our table.

He said, "I heard you were killed. Surely you are not a ghost!"

I laughed and said, "I am very much alive."

I introduced him to my chums and we had quite a chat. Of course he said, "You are all a sight to behold."

I said, "So would you be if you had gone through the ordeal that we have been through."

Here's a description of myself (which was the same as the rest of us):

I had on a Royal Flying Corps uniform and breeches greased from top to bottom, with socks showing, because the Germans had taken my slashed flying boots. I wore the pair of Russian Army private boots laced up the outside given to me by my batman, a German peaked paper hat, and my ripped flying coat (the one that's now in the museum in Ottawa). I knew what I looked like.

I am under the impression we were the first officers to arrive in London, because the crowd made a great fuss over us: we were museum objects.

We had been told to get out of sight, get new uniforms, or get out of London. I bid my pals goodbye and taxied over to Euston Station, where I took a train to Stoke-on-Trent. I had been given an open railway warrant to travel wherever I wanted, and also told to report back in London in two months' time for a medical examination.

The railroad station at Stoke-on-Trent (from an old postcard).

Nancy, her father, and their friends met me at the station and drove me to Hanley. When Nancy's mother saw me, she nearly took a fit. I was such a dirty-looking devil I was not allowed in the house. Instead, I was ordered into their stable yard, where my pockets were emptied and given a searching examination to see that lice were not among my money.

Then I was taken by the men over to a drain and stripped of all my clothes, which were immediately burned in the yard. They then got a hose and caustic soap and they certainly gave me a hosing. When they were satisfied I was vermin-cleaned, I was dried off and a towel wrapped around me, and I was allowed in the house, where I was sent to a bedroom, where all my clothes were laid out.

I had instructed the Air Force that if I was shot down, killed, or captured, to send my belongings to Nancy. I was lucky: I got everything but my hat, which had a large beak, and my tobacco—someone helped themselves. (I was lucky again in that I was able to buy an RAF hat in Hanley. I think it was the only one in that vicinity.)

23

WEDDING BELLS

After I dressed, I was allowed to join the gathering, and what a rejoicing! They had given me up as being killed, especially my sweetheart, Nancy, to whom I was engaged to be married on January 2, 1919.

I got fed up with such a long leave, and asked Nancy's Dad to give me a job around the place. He said, "Okay, come down to the liquor cellar." He pointed to a corner that was piled up to the ceiling with straw taken from around liquor. I removed the new straw—and then ran into decayed boxes and rotten straw.

I had found a fortune!

I got Mr. Ridgway and showed him what I had found. He nearly took a fit, then called Mrs. Ridgway and Nancy.

The whole corner was full of different types of liquor and, of course, champagne. It had been there for ages, perhaps fifty years. People had just moved the top straw and never gone to the wall to remove it all.

Liquor, at that time in Britain, was rationed. One had to make three bottles out of two to meet government regulations. Afterwards it had to be cut in half, two bottles out of one.

The find had to be kept secret. Nancy's father said, "We will have the champagne at the wedding to celebrate Sam's return and his discovery."

My big day approached, and what a fuss they put on; nearly the whole town of Hanley turned out. It was a Church of England wedding, and the building was crowded, because Nancy's people were well-known.

Nancy looked beautiful in her wedding robes and I wore my Royal Air Force uniform. It was quite a sight. Although we were living in the same building, we had been kept apart (and some job it was!) as it is supposed to be bad luck if you see your bride before you view her at the altar.

It was a beautiful service, although I didn't hear it all because the noise from my knees knocking and shaking was a diversion. Was I nervous? Yes! But Nancy was cool and kept me under control.

After I kissed my wife and everyone else had pecked at poor Nancy, we left the church for the photography studio. Everyone was shouting and throwing rice. An old lady got through the crowd and shouted at me to be good to the lassie, and threw an old baby slipper into the car. It landed on my lap. After the service was over, I must say it was the happiest day of my life.

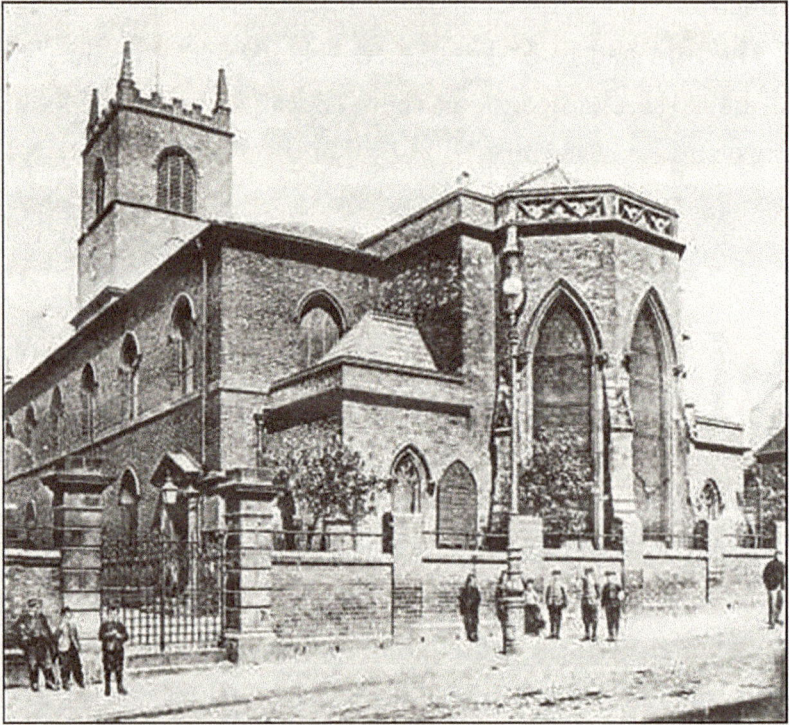

St. John the Evangelist Church in Hanley, ca. 1900, where the wedding most likely took place (from ThePotteries.org).

The evening of the marriage Nancy, Father, and Mother arranged the wedding dinner. What a spread and speech-making! My turn came and I was nearly speechless, but I made a poor attempt. (Who wants to look at the bridegroom? He is a nonentity. It is the bride who gets all the attention.)

Everyone was happy, but the time came for Nancy and me to leave. We were driven to Stoke-on-Trent station. We got into an empty compartment, but just my luck, two businessmen got in after us and started to talk business.

We wished them in the "hot place," but after approximately twenty-five miles they got out. After that, we had the compartment to ourselves all the way to Edinburgh, Scotland. There we were met by relatives and taken to Portobello, where we stayed during our honeymoon.

24

A RETURN TO CHILDHOOD HAUNTS

Portobello was a seaside resort and, of course, the house was a typical seaside establishment, operated by two maiden ladies who were Scottish to the marrow. I remember one instance that did not please us, especially me. A young Scottish officer was staying there, and if he had any meal, he was placed at the head of the long table and all the paraphernalia was set out for him—silver utensils, etc.—while Nancy and I were at the bottom of the table. No one else was there, and we got the common dishes and boarding-house food. He was an officer of the same rank as me, but we never acknowledged one another. We Canadians were not too popular, as we were looked upon as some kind of an aboriginal.

There was a lot of jealousy going on at that time. Our men, soldiers, sailors, and airmen, had acquitted themselves in a wonderful manner, and the American (U.S.) forces had also done a wonderful job: won the war. They didn't mind telling everyone about it ("a worn-out enemy," we said), and of course, the ordinary people did not know we Canadians were part of the British Commonwealth.

To give the Americans their due, I don't think the Allies would have been victorious if they had not received help from the USA: men, goods, and financing. That is my opinion. I was always on excellent terms with the Americans, since we were domiciled in their territory in France (nine squadrons) and the Americans treated us well in their canteens and officers' messes.

The American officers were down-to-earth individuals, and personally I got on first-class with them and all their men, NCOs, and men in the ranks, while I had had enough of the British officers during my training as a cadet. The British officers acted as if they were God's chosen people. They were correct no matter what they said: black was white and white was black, with no shades of colour in between.

We travelled a lot, walking up to the capital and visiting the famous Edinburgh Castle and Sir Walter Scott Monument in Princes Street Gardens. We were shown around by a friendly guard and saw places very few visitors were allowed to see: cells, lookouts, and interior places that were off the beaten path.

Princes Street, Edinburgh, 1924 (from vintag.es).

We went to theatres and concerts and really enjoyed ourselves. We could see the famous bridge on the Firth of Forth, and it came back to me how Mother took Fred and me on a boat trip up the river.

One day we decided to go to Dalkeith and have a look at Langside Cottage. What a disappointment! It was in ruins, and the whole countryside was different from what it was in my childhood and in my mind.

While we were in that part of the country, we decided to

go and look at the old blacksmith shop. It was just a stone's throw from the cottage. There was a horse being shod and the old bellows that I used to pull up and down was blowing away, and Mr. Rennie, Jr. was shoeing a horse and fitting a hot shoe.

When he saw us, he dropped his work and came over to us, and asked us what he could do for us.

I smiled at him, and he gazed at me bewildered. I told him I was Sam Goodfellow.

"You are little Sammy who stayed with the Reids?"

I said, "Yes." I then introduced him to Nancy.

The whole shop stopped work and he shouted, "Alice, Alice, come here. I have a surprise for you."

Alice came running and was flabbergasted when he said, "This is Sammy Goodfellow and his wife Nancy."

Alice, Mrs. Rennie, nearly swooned. She grabbed a hold of me, kissing me. "My little Sammy, and now an Air Force officer!"

Then she hugged Nancy and took us into their house. Mr. Rennie stopped work for the day.

Within a few hours the whole countryside had heard the news, even miles away in the town where Fred and I had gone to school. Mrs. Rennie said, "If only Mother and Father and old Mr. Rennie were living to see you."

They wanted to know where we were living, and we told them Portobello. They said they would phone and tell them we were not coming back, and I said, "No," but we had to stay a few days with them, which we did, and the whole country came to see the wandering boy who had returned to his old home.

Mr. Rennie had bought a second-hand Buick touring car in Edinburgh, taken one hour of driving instruction, and then driven home. He had put the car in one of his sheds and then realized he couldn't, or was scared to, drive on the country roads.

A 1916 Buick touring car (source unknown).

In our conversation, I had told them I had spent fourteen months as a truck driver in France before joining the Royal Flying Corps. That was it! I got the car started and we drove all over the countryside. He would not drive while his family was in the car, so I became the chauffeur.

I then took him out alone and gave him instructions on

driving the Buick and explained the gearshift, etc. Before we left he was an expert driver. He was then able to put his tools in the car and go and shoe horses at the big farms, whereas before he used to take his horse and buggy.

The day came when we had to leave and return to Portobello and Edinburgh. We were all sorry that we had to go. Nancy and I stayed a few days in Edinburgh and then took the train to Nancy's home in Hanley. They were all pleased to see us, and we had lots of visitors.

25

THE CURIOUS CASE OF THE ZOOLOGICAL GARDENS STEAM ENGINE

During my prison leave, Nancy's mother and father had a difficult time keeping me amused. One day they suggested we drive to Chester; it was a walled city, the first I had seen. We walked along the battlemented top of the walls, where the inhabitants in ancient times defended themselves, and also entered their watchtowers.

In flying around England, I had seen from the air Hadrian's Wall, which the Roman emperor Hadrian had built to keep out the barbarian invaders from the north (the Picts and the Scots) between Solway Firth and the mouth of the Tyne.

After enjoying a Chester meal, we drove back to Hanley. It certainly was an enjoyable day. I was always impressed with history, and every time I was in a new country, I always made it a point to look up ancient fortifications, in England, Scotland, France, Belgium, and Germany.

O ne day Mr. Ridgway had to go to Manchester on business, and asked Nancy and me to go along with him. We could visit the Manchester Zoological Gardens, the finest animal zoological gardens in all of Britain. We were game to go.

Mr. Ridgway drove one of his Ford cars, which had the planetary clutch system for changing speed ahead or reverse. We left Hanley and arrived at Manchester about noon. Mr. Ridgway left Nancy and me to window shop while he was transacting his business, and then joined us for lunch.

We then went to the zoo, and after paying an entrance fee, I spied the powerhouse. I could see from the outdoor exhaust pipe that they had a steam engine in operation. We went into the building, met the engineer, and looked at the engine. I said to the engineer, "That is a Corliss Automatic Steam Engine."

He looked at me and said, "How do you know?"

I told him I had served my apprenticeship on steam engines in Canada.

"So, you are an engineer," he said.

I said, "Yes." I went over to the engine and said to him, "My name is on the brass plate." It showed the builder of the engine: SAMPSON JOHN GOODFELLOW.

He would not believe me, and I had to show him my Royal Air Force papers. He couldn't believe it and said, "That is the most peculiar thing I have ever known." Then he asked, "How does my engine run?"

I said, "It seems to operate mechanically very well, but I will go outside and come in and tell you."

A typical Corliss steam engine (engraving from the "Handbook of Corliss Steam Engines" by F.W. Shillito, Jr., 1899).

I went outside, and his exhausts were wonderful, equal-cylinder exhausts from each end, showing steam of a light colour. I then came back in and told him his engine was operating okay.

"Now I believe you that you are a steam expert," he said.

We left him. He was still bewildered at meeting another

Goodfellow. (The name on the plate was one of my ancestors from Birmingham.)

This engine visit brought back to me memories from when I was an apprentice at A.R. Williams. An engineer had been complaining about his engine, bought from A.R. Williams, and I was sent out to see what was wrong.

He was sitting in a nice comfortable engineer's chair, and I asked him what was the matter. He said, "That is why I sent for a mechanic, so you could find out. It is not correct, is it?"

He sure was abrupt. The engineers at that time were that way. They would wear beautiful striped overalls and sit in their chairs with a piece of waste in their hands, for they certainly kept their engines in wonderful shape.

I went out his engine room door, looked at the exhaust, and then came back in, went to the engine, and with a wrench adjusted a screw on the Corliss mechanism and tightened the jam nut. I said, "How does that suit you? It is running fine now. Go outside and look at your exhaust."

He came in and said, "It is okay."

I was just lucky. I could have made it worse. If I had, I would have put the adjustment back where it was and then known it was the opposite end, but that is the chance you take when you can't shut the engine down.

We went through the zoo and Mr. Ridgway had the time of his life calling the monkeys Sam or Nancy.

Of course, him being our senior, we had to take the jokes and laugh along with him.

A keeper with chimps at a "tea-party" in 1920 at the Belle Vue Zoological Gardens in Manchester (Manchester City Council Image Archives).

We finally left Manchester before it became dark. It was a wonderful outing. Mr. Ridgway told Mrs. Ridgway about the episode with the engine and, of course, said he'd met some of Sam's relatives in the monkey cage.

26

"I WISH WE HAD MORE OF YOUR CALIBER"

Before leaving the Air Force headquarters in London on my prison two-month leave, I was instructed to return at a certain date for medical examination and posting, if I was medically fit. I was walking along the Strand when whom should I run into but Roy Byrnes, a pilot and our old baseball pitcher. We had quite a chat and it was the same old story; he'd thought I was killed.

Of course, the Air Force casualties were mentioned in the paper, and if you were in the missing column it was presumed you were dead. Nancy and her folks were certain I was killed. They went to a fortune teller, and were told, "You couldn't kill that devil. He is alive and trying to escape."

I bid Byrnes good-bye and never saw him again.

I reported at headquarters, and after a lot of paperwork I

was sent up to be medically examined. The old military doctor gave me a wonderful examination. When he was through he said, "I am going to send you to a hospital for a rest period and further examination. What happened to you in France?"

"Doctor, my history is on my paper, which you have."

"Yes, it will be there, but I didn't read it." He got the paper and read it very thoroughly. I watched him nodding. Then he said, "Boy, you have been through hell, and you have been very lucky as a soldier and airman."

I said, "Sir, I don't want to go to a hospital. Send me on duty and I will soon be okay."

"Yes," he said, "with your luck, I believe you." He then wrote on my papers a few remarks about my physical condition and okayed me for duty.

I thanked him and reported at the correct quarters and was given my destination papers and railroad warrants. I then was told to report at Netheravon for flying duty. This was okay with me, because I got lieutenant and flying pay, which I needed now I was a married man and needed all the cash I could get.

I finally arrived at the Netheravon Aerodrome at night. I went to the orderly room—and I was in trouble again. When I entered the room, a young pup of a Royal Air Force ground lieutenant shouted at me, demanding why I did not salute.

I asked who the hell he was talking to and told him I would knock his block off if he talked to me that way, and also told him you didn't salute in an orderly room.

He said, "Don't you see the OC here?"

I said, "Where? I don't see anybody!"

With that, the OC, who was hiding behind a stove, said it was, "Okay, Canada."

They had been notified I would arrive that day. It was after dinner and he had imbibed too much and was the worse for wear. He and I laughed it off, and I shook hands with the colonel.

Officers' quarters at Netheravon Aerodrome in 2013 (Stuart Logan / Southwestern corner of Netheravon Camp / CC BY-SA 2.0).

The lieutenant gave me particulars of my sleeping quarters, mess meal hours, and other matters. I was then told to report at the colonel's orderly room at 10 a.m. tomorrow.

I went to my quarters and then to the officers' mess, and who the devil did I run into but Captain Montmorency, the individual who had gotten me into all the trouble at Bath when I was a cadet. Was he surprised some! He put out his hand to shake mine, and shook it, then said a few words.

I didn't answer him and walked past him. He knew that I had not forgotten.

I had a brandy and soda and then went to bed. It was a four-bed room. My roommates were a South African infantry officer who had transferred to the Air Force to be trained as a pilot, and two officer pilots from the Thirty-Fifth Officers' Training Class; Lieutenant Jost, a Nova Scotian, and Lieutenant Searle, a Manitoban. The next morning when I went to have breakfast who should I run into but Heiny Rogers, a pal of mine from Regina, who was in the same Thirty-Fifth Class as my roommates.

After breakfast, I reported to the orderly room and ran into the same orderly room lieutenant I had had words with the night before, but he was a different individual: he had read my papers.

He said, "The OC will see you at once. He has been

waiting for you and told me to usher you in as soon as you arrived."

I went into the colonel's private office and saluted. He told me to take a chair. When I sat down, he said, "I was a little under the weather last night."

I said, "I did not notice."

He looked at me then said, "You're okay." He said, "You have come here highly recommended and I have instructions to put you in charge of the mechanical department. Lieutenant Dry is acting at the present time.

"We have three squadrons here: two of them are being disbanded. The best personnel will be in one squadron; the rest will be discharged."

He said, "This morning I have read your papers, and you certainly have had an eventful life, both as a truck driver and as a cadet and officer. The guardian angel must be looking after you. You have been through enough to be dead several times."

He asked me about my life at Vimy and Passchendaele and I gave him a short description. He said, "What did you think when you were being anti-aircraft shelled? They had your range and shot off parts of your plane, and the tracers were sprinkling your plane."

I told him I just said, "Good-bye, Goodfellow, they got you this time," then I hit the ground.

"You're to be admired the way you conducted yourself at the German headquarters when they wanted information," he said. "The German captain would have hit you and you would have hit him back if the German general had not stopped questioning. You would have been shot."

I said, "They would not get information from me even if they had threatened to shoot me."

He said, "I wish we had more of your caliber."

I thanked him, got up, saluted, and left.

27

THE CANADIANS RUN AMOK

Then I reported to Lieutenant Dry. His promotion had not come through when the war ended. He was still a lieutenant, not knowing he was going to be discharged as not suitable personnel for the permanent Air Force, but he insisted on being called Captain Dry by his subordinates, which included me. It did not bother me. I would call him any name he wished.

The building that Captain Dry occupied was some distance from the headquarters and the officers' mess, but it was on the main road. I soon found the mechanical office with its occupants. I informed Captain Dry that the OC had sent me to be his assistant.

I don't know when he felt that his days in the RAF were finished. He asked me a few questions regarding my training and my duty since joining the Army and the Air Force. I knew right away that he was unsuited for the job he was occupying.

He told me to look around and acquaint myself with the office, etc., and then disappeared. I knew from the action of the staff that he was not liked; they gave a sign of relief.

I looked around the office and asked a few questions. I then visited the shops and met the regimental sergeant-major and the rest of the NCOs. They were very cordial, and during our conversation they learned I was no novice like Dry.

Noon hour came, and I went to the officers' mess and met all the Canadians of the Thirty-Fifth Officers' Training Class. They were glad that a Canadian with some seniority had come to Netheravon.

D uring my time at this aerodrome, the railway employees went on strike. It was a terrible thing to do just when the war was over and Britain had not gotten organized to peace-time control; but they did not take into account that they were dealing with a tough secretary of state, Winston Churchill. He organized all the available trucks and got volunteer drivers for the forces. The populace was with him and the government.

All the Canadian officers in Class Thirty-Five volunteered to drive trucks. Their run was from London to Wales, carrying food from the London docks to all the places en route. I was in a terrible position, because I belonged to the International Association of Machinists, and if it became known in Canada that I was strike breaking, it would go against me. My chums, Jost and Searle, knew I had driven a truck in France, so to them I explained the situation. Everything worked out to my satisfaction: I was given an office job routing the trucks, drivers, etc. The strike did not last long, because the union officials knew that Churchill would stand no nonsense.

Military trucks in convoy during the 1919 railway strike (source unknown)

The CO did not know what to do with the class, since flying had stopped, so he put them to digging ditches to run off the rain, since there was no drainage on the aerodrome. I used to have a good time kidding them when they were "working," leaning on their shovels. I used to say when I was going to the office, "Come on boys, stop leaning on the shovels."

You can imagine what they called me; they knew, me being a Canadian, they could get away with it. If I had been an English officer, they would have just sworn under their breath.

The job didn't last long, as one night we had a terrible storm that came from Plymouth. Nearly all the airplanes that were left on the aerodrome, especially the Avro training planes, were blown around like leaves. It was lucky that the Handley Pages were in the hangars.

The day came when the OC received instructions from London headquarters that the Thirty-Fifth Class be sent to Liverpool to embark and return to Canada.

Then word came through that a mistake had been made. They had been receiving flying pay as well as second-lieutenant pay. Now they had to return all the flying pay that they had received. It was impossible for them to do that, since most of them had been living very high, and the money was spent. How they got out of that predicament I don't know. The fellows were very mad about this order, but they decided to have a farewell party. The organizer went around and collected two pounds from every Canadian, me included.

They took over the mess sitting room. No one except a Canuck could enter that day. They purchased Scotch, rye, gin, etc., got a big porcelain washbasin, and poured the liquor in up to the brim, along with some fruit juices. We had dinner, then went in to the party.

It was some party, and the mixture out of the basin was like dynamite. I had one drink and could see things were getting rough. Me being the senior officer, I decided to get out.

I got in touch with my roommates, Jost and Searle, told them I was leaving, and advised them to do likewise. They agreed. I said, "I will go first. They won't miss me; then you leave one at a time."

We three finally got out and went to our sleeping quarters, which was the next-door building. We could hear the rumpus in the mess. Our roommate was with us.

All at once, everything went quiet, for about a quarter of an hour.

They had left the mess and had gone to the ammunition building, where flares, rockets, and Very pistols with three different colours were kept under lock and key, as these were dangerous. Did they have a wonderful time setting off rockets and flares and shooting Very pistols! It got so bad that a state of emergency was called. The commanding officer had the fire alarm sounded and troops half-dressed responded. They chased all the class to their quarters and everything became quiet.

Then we three went to sleep, glad that we were not in it.

The next morning, we three got up early and went into the party room. What a sight! The piano was lying on its back; chairs were sticking out horizontally from the plasterboard walls; crockery, glass, and furniture were broken. It was terrible that a gang could do such a thing.

London HQ heard about it from the aerodrome, and instructions were given to get the class on the train for Liverpool at once and then on their way to Canada. They ordered the class to pay for the damage. It was decided that two pounds from every Canadian would be sufficient, so it cost me another two pounds, but I was questioned and I proved that Jost, Searle, and I had left before the trouble started. My other roommate, the South African, was our witness: he had watched the trouble from our sleeping quarters along with us three.

Still, four pounds was a big price to pay for one drink!

I asked Jost and Searle what had caused all the trouble, and they told me it was the order to return flying pay. They had quite flying before I reached the aerodrome.

The next day the class left. I was sorry to see my chums leave.

I kept in touch for a number of years with Lieutenant Jost, until he died, but lost touch with Lieutenant Searle.

28

OFFICER IN CHARGE

There I was, the only Canadian at the aerodrome. After breakfast, I went to our office and did some work. I heard a few remarks about the rowdy Canadian, and, of course, when I went to the mess for lunch I was looked upon as a black sheep or a cannibal.

A few days passed while I was getting the hang of their system, which was terrible. A pad of letters would come about a certain thing. If you did not know anything about it, you got rid of it quick and sent it to someone else with a note attached, telling the officer you sent it to, "For Your Attention, Sir," and signing it. He did likewise.

One day Captain Dry came to the office in tears and I said, "What happened?" (Of course, I knew.)

He said, "I have just received my discharge papers from the OC and they came from HQ London. I am in a terrible mess. I have just bought a motor car, a Rolls Royce, on part payment. I'm engaged to the doctor's daughter—we were to be married in a month—and I have no training to get a job in civilian life to keep her in the style she has been used to."

I asked him what he worked at before he joined the Air Force, and he told me he had had a menial job working in a sporting goods shop repairing bicycles, and had no education to fit him for an advanced position. I asked him how he had ever got into the Flying Corps, as we Canadians had to have a certain standard.

He said he had bluffed them, and now he had to pay the price.

I told him the only thing he could do was to see the doctor, the girl's father, and tell him what had happened in detail, and then see the doctor's daughter. He must have taken my advice, for he disappeared, and I never saw him again.

I then became the officer in charge. There had been a lot of stealing going on, as well as pilots taking aeroplanes without consent of the OC. I called a meeting of all my NCOs and office staff and then laid down the rules.

I put the regimental sergeant major over all the NCO jobs that I allotted. I gave each sergeant and corporal a certain job and told them I didn't want any damn excuses: no aeroplane of our squadron was to go off the ground without my consent.

The sergeant whom I had placed in charge of planes was to take some of his men and take every watch out of every plane and bring them to me. I locked them up and kept the key.

I put some NCOs in charge of the shop, some in charge of the tool room, and some in charge of the spare engines inside and outside in crates. (We had a large consignment of Liberty engines from the USA that had never been uncrated.)

Stocks were taken and we had a meeting every morning to see if the system was working satisfactorily. It was. I saw the OC and told him that I would not let one of our planes leave without him giving his okay. That pleased him, because he had been in hot water about wreckage.

One day an officer came to our office with an okay from the OC to have a plane. He informed me that there was no watch in the plane and he wanted one.

I said, "Have you a wrist watch?"

He put out his arm and showed me his watch.

"You don't get a watch. Use the one you have."

He said, "I will see the OC and he will make you put one in the plane."

I said, "Who is stopping you? Good-bye."

I didn't hear any more and no one asked for a watch again.

They were disbanding one of the squadrons, and the OC of this squadron sent a corporal down to see me to get a clearance for his planes and workshop, etc. I read the letter that he wanted me to sign. I told the corporal that I would not sign the paper and he left.

After a while, he came back and told me his OC said I had to sign it. I sent him away again, and down he came again and told me his OC, a major or a colonel, ordered me to sign the paper.

I told him the same thing; that I would not sign the letter.

The OC came to me himself, roaring like a wild bull, and ordered me to sign the release.

I said, "No, sir, I will not sign the release."

He got quite hostile. What he wouldn't do to me for disobeying a senior officer!

Then all at once he got hold of himself, and in a nice manner asked me why I would not sign his release.

I told him in a nice manner that I did not have the authority to sign any releases.

He said, "You are in charge and you must have signed when you took over."

I said, "No."

He said, "You mean to say they gave you this job without signing?"

I said, "Yes." I told him to go and see the head OC, and I never saw him again.

The airmen were getting to be a restless bunch, because the poor mechanics were getting discharged and the good mechanics were getting taken on the permanent staff.

One day I wanted some information from my shop corporal and went to the shop. I asked the men at the door where he was. I got an answer that didn't please me, so I walked down the length of the shop. The men did everything but trip me.

I finally got to where he was, and there he was, shaving himself on army time. He saw my reflection in his mirror and turned, flabbergasted, with his face covered with soap, and saluted me. I asked him what I wanted to know, saluted, said, "Carry on," and left. I never let on I saw him shaving, for if I had, I would have had to report him.

From that day, I had all the loyalty of the men. The Canadian was okay.

I had no trouble during my period of operating the mechanical and office part of my new job, but one day we missed an aeroplane—one had been taken without permission.

Before the day was out we were informed it had come down at an aerodrome near Cambridge, out of gasoline. We dispatched an aeroplane the next day along with two officers to return the plane, along with the officer who had taken the plane.

29

A NEW LIFE BEGINS

After a period of time, I was ordered to report to the OC orderly room and was asked if I would consider joining the permanent Royal Air Force. They had found out that I was an engineer and a mechanical draftsman. The OC informed me that the instructions had come from London. He told me what a good life it was and great advantage to me, since I would be promoted in rank.

I explained to him I could not give an answer until I had thought the matter over and spoken to my wife. After a few days, I told him that I wanted my discharge and return to Canada, because I had promised a former employer that I was returning and they had asked me to come as quickly as I could. He was very sorry to hear my decision and said he would notify London HQ at once.

A couple of days passed, and again I was told to go to the

orderly room. The OC informed me that I was being transferred to the Central Flying School at Upavon. He told me I
was to go there as a lecturer on aviation.

I packed up, not too sorry to leave, and was driven to the
school, which was the most advanced school at that time.

After a few days, I was told to report to the orderly room.
Again, the OC told me that HQ London wanted me to join
the permanent Air Force. If I would, they would promote me
to field rank (major).

This was a greatly tempting offer and I hesitated before
giving an answer. I asked the OC if I could have a few days to
go and interview my wife and her people, my father and
mother having passed away. I said I would like the opinion
of my wife's people because they were living in England.

He consented, and gave me a pass for a few days and train
warrants. I left and went to Hanley. Nancy, her mother and
father, and I talked the matter over very carefully.

Her parents would have preferred their daughter to stay
in England (the labour trouble was in progress in Winnipeg
and had had a big write up in Britain), but they left the
matter of me staying in the Air Force up to my wife, Nancy.
Nancy decided I should get my discharge and we would go
to Regina, Canada.

I returned to Upavon and spoke to the OC, refusing the
offer to stay in the Royal Air Force. He stated I was making a
mistake and informed me that I would be placed in reserve
for ten years, and that if I was wanted I had to return to
England at once.

I could understand why they wanted trained personnel, since the cream of British manhood had been killed or wounded. The young flyers had left school to join the forces and had no practical training.

However, my friends in the Canadian forces and in the Royal Canadian Mounted Police said we made the correct decision. I was not suited for life in the forces because I could not stand discipline. They had plenty in the forces who were ignorant of their calling. Brave? Yes, but they lacked training and business knowledge. There was a lot of jealousy, because the Canadians had made a wonderful name for themselves.

The OC gave orders for me to have a short leave and provided railway warrants for Nancy and myself, and also gave written orders for us to be at Liverpool at a certain date to report to the Air Force officer in charge to board the *Metagama*.

I phoned Nancy, and they met me at Stoke-on-Trent for my last Air Force holiday in England. We had several trips around Staffordshire, but time went very quickly, and the time came for us to leave for Liverpool.

Mr. and Mrs. Ridgway drove us to our destination, and the time came for us to go aboard. Amid tears on both sides, we said goodbye. It was very hard for Nancy, since she had led a very sheltered life, but she took it very bravely.

The boat pulled out, and we waved good-bye to old England.

Nancy and I were assigned to a four-bunk cabin; the other couple was of the fast set, and we were just the opposite. The officer came to me and asked if I would change with a couple across the aisle. I said we would, and the other couple was of our type and so were lovely to meet. Their names were Harold and Lilian Broadberry. He was a navigator in 213 Squadron, Independent Air Force.

It was a very congenial trip. We had lots of fun about who was going to their bunk first. We got over that difficulty by having the ladies go to bed first, while we went for a walk on deck. Then when we returned, it was the girls' turn to kid us, and they would pretend that they were peeking. We got on fine, and they have been our friends since that day.

They went to Fillmore, Saskatchewan. After a few years they moved to Wisconsin and started a dairy farm, which was very successful, but a few years ago Harold passed away. Their daughter got married and visited us when we lived in Calgary.

We stayed in Toronto with Mr. and Mrs. Dean and their two daughters, who were friends of my mother. I knew Mr. Dean when I was a youngster. He was an original brass molder and gave me two brass book ends of Romeo and Juliet, which I still have.

When he got older, he started an animal and feed store on Yonge Street in Toronto. We kids used to go and see him, specially the parrots. We would say, "Polly wants a cracker," and the birds would join in the remark.

The brass bookends of Romeo and Juliet.

Nancy and I were in Toronto on the twelfth of July and watched the Orange Parade on Yonge Street, opposite Carlton Street. I explained the reason for the parade: the Battle of the Boyne in Ireland, which was a part of a religious war. The Boyne is a river, seventy miles long, in eastern Ireland. William III defeated James II near there in 1690, and the Protestants who belong to the Orange lodges still celebrate the occasion.

I called on a few of my school chums and introduced them to my Nancy, but the girls who were not married did not give me much of a welcome. We stayed a few days, and then we were on our way to Regina.

What a mistake it was coming at that time of the year! The Regina Exhibition had just started. We did not have a place to lay our heads, but a Regina chum came to my rescue. Jack and Mildred Thorton put us up during the Exhibition, and then we found three vacant rooms on Thirteen Block Retallack Street, Jack and Gora Braham's home.

It was a lovely start.

THE END

ABOUT SAM AND NANCY GOODFELLOW

SAM AND NANCY GOOD-
FELLOW took up permanent
residence in Regina, where
Sam worked in machine engi-
neering and eventually
became president of Western
Machine and Engineering
Ltd.

The Goodfellows became
great supporters of the arts in
their adopted city. Sam was

Sam and Nancy Goodfellow, 1960s.

elected to the Board of Direc-
tors of Regina Little Theatre in 1953 and eventually served
two years as president. He established the Regina Little
Theatre Annual Award for most valuable contribution to

RLT, an award that is still presented annually and is known as the "Sammy" in his honour. He also provided funds for the establishment of an annual scholarship for an RLT member.

Sam was also a patron of the Saskatchewan Region of the Dominion Drama Festival for more than thirty years, beginning in 1948, and was a patron of the Dominion Drama Festival from 1955 to 1968.

In addition, Sam served as chairman of the Regina Symphony Orchestra Management Committee for two years, and also chaired the Symphony's finance committee. As a patron of the Regina Symphony Orchestra, he assisted in paying off its accumulated debt.

Sam was also a member (and eventually treasurer) of the citizens' committee that planned and realized the design and construction of the Saskatchewan Centre of the Arts (today the Conexus Arts Centre), the province's premiere performance space for music, dance, and major theatrical productions.

With Sam's encouragement, Nancy took both voice and piano lessons at the Conservatory of Music after her arrival in Regina. She became an acclaimed recitalist, and a member of the first formation of the Elizabethan Singers, playing Darke Hall in many concerts and entertaining crowds as a vocalist. She was also a member of the Regina Music Club and active in bringing concert artists to Regina.

Nancy also served on the Regina Little Theatre executive, where she was responsible for obtaining patron donations and arranging social events. She was a member of the regional executive of the Dominion Drama Festival and represented the Saskatchewan region at national meetings of the board of governors.

Sam was eventually named a life member of Regina Little Theatre. A room in the RLT's former building on Saskatchewan Drive was furnished as a lounge and called the Sam and Nancy Room; the green room in Regina Little Theatre's current space in the Regina Performing Arts Centre still displays Sam's and Nancy's photos and biography.

The Goodfellows provided a fund to the University of Saskatchewan, Regina Campus, to establish several permanent annual scholarships: two for post-graduate studies in science, and two in music (vocal and piano) leading to a music degree; they also endowed scholarships for the College of Notre Dame in Wilcox. They provided a fund to assist young people into the ministry of the Presbyterian Church of Canada, and increased the fund to assist the ladies' section in assisting young women to enter church service.

Sam and Nancy had one daughter, Alice, born in 1922. She became a medical doctor, graduating from the University of Toronto in 1946, and practiced as a pediatrician in both Toronto and Regina.

Nancy died in 1974. In 1975 Sam provided a fund to the science department of the University of Saskatchewan to assist professors to visit or obtain up-to-date information on subjects in other parts of the world. In 1976 he provided money to the Regina Musical Club for the annual Anne Owen (Nancy) Goodfellow, presented at the club's discretion, in memory of his wife.

In all, the Goodfellows endowed eight scholarships for the Saskatchewan Music Festival Association, and five for the Conservatory of Music.

In 1978, Sam received an honourary Doctor of Laws degree from the University of Regina in recognition of his many inventions for the grain-handling industry, his involvement in community projects, and his philanthropy.

He died in 1979.

ABOUT THE EDITOR

EDWARD WILLETT is the author of more than sixty books of science fiction, fantasy, and non-fiction for adults, young adults, and children. *Marseguro* (DAW Books) won the Aurora Award (honouring the best in Canadian science fiction and fantasy) for Best Long-Form Work in English in 2009, and the

Edward Willett

second book in the *Double Helix* duology, *Terra Insegura*, was short-listed the following year. His young adult fantasy *Spirit Singer* (Tyche Books) won the Regina Book Award at the 2002 Saskatchewan Book Awards. Several other of his books have been shortlisted for both the Aurora and the Saskatchewan Book Awards.

Willett's most recent novel for DAW, *Worldshaper*, launches a new fantasy/science fiction series. Other recent titles include the *Masks of Aygrima* trilogy for DAW (written as E.C. Blake) and the five-book *Shards of Excalibur* YA fantasy series for Coteau Books. His non-fiction runs the gamut from science books to biographies to history, including *Historic Walks of Regina and Moose Jaw* and *Government House, Regina, Saskatchewan: An Illustrated History.*

Born in Silver City, New Mexico, Ed moved to Saskatchewan with his parents from Texas when he was eight years old, and grew up in Weyburn, where his father taught at Western Christian College. He earned a B.A. in journalism from Harding University in Searcy, Arkansas, and returned to Weyburn to being his career at the weekly *Weyburn Review*, first as a reporter/photographer (and columnist and cartoonist), and eventually as news editor. He moved to Regina in 1988 to become communications officer for the then-fledgling Saskatchewan Science Centre, and became a full-time freelance writer in 1993.

For two decades Ed wrote a weekly science column that appeared in the *Regina Leader Post* and assorted other newspapers; an audio version also ran weekly on CBC Radio's *Afternoon Edition* in Regina for seventeen of those years. He has also appeared on CBC-TV nationally to talk about science topics.

In addition to writing, Ed is a professional actor and

singer who has performed in numerous plays, musicals, and operas, as well as singing with various choirs, including the Canadian Chamber Choir, and, currently, the Prairie Chamber Choir. He lives in Sam and Nancy Goodfellow's former home with his wife, Margaret Anne Hodges, P. Eng. (Sam and Nancy's granddaughter), a past president of the Association of Professional Engineers and Geoscientists of Saskatchewan, their teenaged daughter (Sam and Nancy's great-granddaughter), Alice, and their black Siberian cat, Shadowpaw.

You can find Ed online at www.edwardwillett.com.

CPSIA information can be obtained
at www.ICGtesting.com
Printed in the USA
LVHW022034191118
597646LV00006B/1002/P

9 781999 382766